Supportive Conversations on Facebook Timelines

T0353042

The emergence of social networking sites, like Facebook, and people's engagement with one another through them is a relatively under-researched area for discourse analysis. The content of the book revolves around Discourse Topic Management which is under the theme of Discourse Analysis. It is written to extend the very limited literature in the area of Discourse Topic, especially for the discourse which takes place on social networking sites. This study discusses the characteristics of topical actions employed by English language teachers and their Facebook Friends in managing supportive conversations which take place on Timelines. In addition to employing new strategies, enabled by the particular features of the site, the teachers and their Friends also creatively adapt the strategies used in face-to-face conversations to manage their online conversations, thus contributing to the emergence of unique characteristics of discourse topic management in the context of social networking sites. The book brings together the existing frameworks of Discourse Topic Management, which are previously applied in the context of face-to-face conversations, and synthesizes the frameworks for a more comprehensive model into examining the conversations which take place on Facebook Timelines. The novelty of this book lies in its synthesized framework, the recontextualization of the framework for online conversations and the theoretical extension based on the data analysis presented in each chapter.

Since people's engagement with social networking sites is an emerging behaviour, this timely book provides insights into the phenomenon and also proposes a comprehensive analytical framework for other researchers interested in similar contexts.

Radzuwan Ab. Rashid is Deputy Dean of Research and Development in the Faculty of Languages and Communication, Universiti Sultan Zainal Abidin (UniSZA), Malaysia.

Kamariah Yunus is Senior Lecturer at the Centre of English Language Studies, Faculty of Languages and Communication, Universiti Sultan Zainal Abidin (UniSZA), Malaysia.

Zanirah Wahab is Lecturer at Universiti Sultan Zainal Abidin (UniSZA), Malaysia.

Supportive Conversations on Facebook Timelines

Discourse Topic Management

Radzuwan Ab. Rashid, Kamariah Yunus and Zanirah Wahab

Routledge
Taylor & Francis Group

LONDON AND NEW YORK

First published 2018
by Routledge

2 Park Square, Milton Park, Abingdon, Oxfordshire OX14 4RN
52 Vanderbilt Avenue, New York, NY 10017

Routledge is an imprint of the Taylor & Francis Group, an informa business

First issued in paperback 2019

British Library Cataloguing-in-Publication Data
A catalogue record for this book is available from the British Library

Library of Congress Cataloging-in-Publication Data
A catalog record for this book has been requested

ISBN: 978-1-138-48245-6 (hbk)
ISBN: 978-0-367-89311-8 (pbk)

Typeset in Times New Roman
by Apex CoVantage, LLC

Contents

Figures

Acknowledgements

The authors thank Dr. Mary Bailey and Dr. Jane Evison from the University of Nottingham, United Kingdom, for their meaningful guidance during the course of the study. This book would not be possible without their valuable comments in the process of conceptualizing discourse topic management, which is the main theme of this book.

The authors also thank the Ministry of Higher Education and Universiti Sultan Zainal Abidin (UniSZA), Malaysia, for funding this research project under the SLAB/SLAI scheme.

1 Discourse topic

Towards understanding topical actions on Timelines

Discourse can be defined as 'sets of linguistic materials that have a degree of coherence in their content and organization and which perform constructive functions in broadly defined social contexts' (Coyle, 2006, p. 370). In the study of discourse, there have been many attempts to construct theoretical concepts of 'topic'. Brown and Yule (1983), amongst the key authors who discuss the notion of topic, admit that it is a concept 'very difficult to pin down' (p. 68), and it is the most 'frequently used, unexplained, term in the analysis of discourse' (p. 70). Gardner (1987) agrees with Brown and Yule when he states there are 'considerable problems in formally identifying topic' (p. 129).

It is helpful here to distinguish two different notions of topic: sentential topic and discourse topic. Sentential topic is the subject of the sentence and is expressed by a noun or noun phrase (Brown and Yule, 1983). For instance, in the sentence 'John kicks the ball', the topic (the subject) is 'John' whilst 'kicks the ball' is known as the predicate. The sentential topic is also known as the 'theme' or the 'given' in a sentence, in contrast to the 'rheme' or 'new' (Gardner, 1987, p. 134). However, this chapter is not concerned with the structure of linguistic units comparable to simple sentences; its primary interest is in the notion of 'topic' as 'what is being talked about' in a conversation. It is this 'aboutness of talk' that Keenan and Schieffelin (1976, p. 380) term 'discourse topic' that is the concern of this chapter and the book as a whole.

The notion of a discourse topic itself is unclear, as different discourse analysts have different perceptions of what constitutes a discourse topic and how to identify the topic of any particular discourse. Gardner (1987) claims 'none of the definitions of topic is entirely satisfactory' (p. 136). For instance, Keenan and Schieffelin (1976) suggest that 'discourse topic is not a simple NP [noun phrase], but a proposition about which some claim is made or elicited' (p. 380). Hence, Keenan and Schieffelin suggest that a discourse topic is equivalent to a title that sums up a fragment of conversational discourse. Brown and Yule (1983) criticize this notion of discourse topic as 'too simplistic' (p. 71), as Keenan and Schieffelin seem to suggest that there is always a single correct expression of 'the topic' that sums up any text. Brown and Yule argue that the topic of any text can be expressed in different ways (for instance, a summary which does not include any actual word used in the text), and 'each different way of expressing the topic will effectively represent a different judgment of what is being written (or talked about) in a text' (p. 73).

Despite the ambiguity of the notion of discourse topic, Bublitz's (1988) definition of discourse topic provides useful insights into understanding the discursive construction of social support. According to Bublitz, discourse topic refers 'not only to the subject of the (section of the) conversation analyzed (the subject matter, what it is about) but also to *what was done* with it' (p. 22 – original emphasis). In other words, discourse topic is 'the outcome of a process of ascription in which a subject is linked to a complex speech act pattern' (p. 25). Zitzen (2004) and Rashid (2016) argue that looking at discourse topic from Bublitz's perspective enables conversation analysts to relate formal structures of topic organization with participants' actions.

Bublitz's (1988) conceptualization of discourse topic, which should include speech acts, can be associated with the concept of 'move' proposed by Sinclair and Coulthard (1975) in their exchange structure theory. Moves, according to Sinclair and Coulthard, are made up of acts, which are 'the lowest rank of discourse' (p. 27). The exchange structure theory will not be discussed in detail because the primary concern of this chapter is the 'about-ness' of the teachers' postings on a social networking site rather than on the exchange structure of the postings.

In line with Brown and Yule (1983), Bublitz (1988) suggests discourse topic can be subject to variation arising from different interpretations. One example of discourse topic as an answer to the question 'what have you been talking about' highlighted by Bublitz is 'we have been CONSIDER-ING which films to go and see' (p. 35 – original emphasis). The speech act *considering* is linked to the subject *films* to form the discourse topic.

Gardner (1987) and Bublitz (1988) draw attention to topical development and topical actions to identify the discourse topic. Topical development, as proposed by Gardner, includes (1) topic introduction, (2) topic continuation, (3) topic shift, (4) topic recycling, (5) topic reintroduction, and (6) topic change. On the other hand, Bublitz's topical actions for handling discourse topics include (1) introducing a topic, (2) changing a topic, (3) digressing from a topic, (4) shifting a topic, and (5) closing a topic.

Comparative analysis of Gardner (1987) and Bublitz (1988) reveals many similarities, although the authors do not cite each other in their work. For instance, under the topical action of introducing a topic, Bublitz combines the topical development of topic reintroduction highlighted by Gardner. Even though Bublitz provides a clearer explanation than Gardner for the divisions between each topical action, he does not elaborate on 'topic continuation' as discussed by Gardner. Therefore, to overcome these shortcomings, Gardner's topical development and Bublitz's topical actions are combined to provide a comprehensive analytical lens by adding Gardner's topic continuation to Bublitz's list of topical actions.

The analytic lens used in examining teachers' postings on Timelines is mainly based on Bublitz's (1988) topical actions. However, we argue that topic continuation (Gardner, 1987) should be added to the list of topical actions proposed by Bublitz to provide a more comprehensive analysis. Excluding topic continuation will exclude insights into how a particular topic subject is developed and expanded before it is changed, shifted, digressed or closed by the participants.

The synthesis of topical actions used as the analytic lens in this book is shown in Figure 1.1.

Towards understanding topical actions on Timelines

The concept of topic handling, or what Bublitz (1988, p. 40) refers to as 'topical actions', has its root in face-to-face conversation analysis. Nonetheless, it provides a useful basis for understanding the interactions that

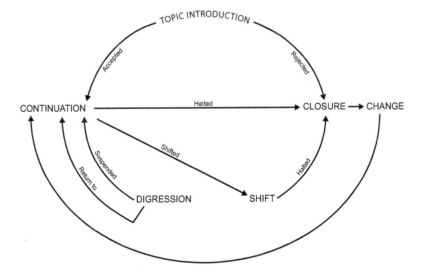

Figure 1.1 The synthesis of topical actions
Source: Based on Bublitz (1988) and Gardner (1987).

occur on Timelines, and we therefore adapted this to use as an analytical framework. The decision to adapt the topical action was also influenced by the scarcity of research that focuses on the notion of topic in online interactions, especially research involving SNS, such as Facebook. Most reports of research into online interaction that use the term 'topic' seem to understand the term as synonymous with 'theme', as used in thematic analysis (e.g. Beaudin, 1999; Zubiaga, Spina and Martínez, 2011) and therefore leave the topical actions in talk unscrutinized.

The conversations on Timelines consist of two elements: Status updates and Comments. The Status needs to be updated by the Profile owner before Friends can leave Comments and then engage in a conversation. Therefore, a Status update can be said to be the 'opening move' (Sinclair and Coulthard, 1992, p. 22) in talk, whereas the first Comment that follows is the second move, the second Comment is the third move and so forth. Based on Bublitz's (1988) notion of discourse topic, the acts that constitute these moves must be taken into consideration when highlighting topics in the talk. For example, the Profile owner might introduce the first topic in the Status update (opening move) by criticizing (act) a newly introduced educational policy.

The way Comments are presented on Timelines seems similar to the concept of a linear array of 'one-turn-at-a-time' allocation in face-to-face conversation (Sacks, Schegloff and Jefferson, 1974, p. 729), as posting Comments is an asynchronous action and the Comments posted are listed one after another. Nonetheless, the concept of sequential relations in face-to-face discourse (Schegloff, 1972) cannot be wholly applied as a basis for examining the topical actions on Timelines. This is because in a long series of Comments, the earlier Comments will be hidden in Facebook. For instance, in the conversation shown in Figure 1.2, there are 28 Comments altogether, but the first 24 Comments are hidden. By default, only the four latest Comments are shown. Therefore, Friends who wish to follow the conversation from the beginning need to click the 'View more comments' link. Because the existing Comments are not otherwise displayed, there is the possibility that a new participant in the conversation might not click the link and will merely leave a Comment in response to the Status update and the latest four Comments displayed.

Because only four Comments are by default displayed on Timelines, it is hard to determine whether the fifth Comment performs any topical action related to the earlier Comments or only to the latest four Comments. Referring to the example in Figure 1.2, it would be incorrect to report that Comment 29 left by a Friend attempts to perform, for instance, the action of reintroducing the topic introduced in Comment 24 because we do not know whether the Friend clicked the 'View 24 more comments' link to access the

Teaching on weekend. Need to provide show cause letter if not coming to work

Like · Comment · Share

and 8 others like this.

View 24 more comments

what I meant with fire is using politics. The opposition loves this kind of thing. They will definitely want to highlight this problem for political mileage. It's dirty, but it seems like playing with dirt is the only way to go in Malaysia. Sad but true. My opinion.
February 20 at 9:06am · Like · 1

Ai yo yo
February 20 at 9:28am · Like · 1

that's what happen when u go up in the admin ladder not bec of ur hardwork but thru political connection. And they flaunt that fact by victimising tchrs n threatening with that surat tunjuk sebab
February 20 at 10:53am · Like · 2

I feel for you
February 20 at 10:56am · Like · 1

Write a comment...

Figure 1.2 Hidden Comments on Timelines

earlier phase of the conversation. Therefore, the topical actions on Timelines should be analyzed in four sequence blocks of Comments, which we refer to as a *four-sequence exchange* of Timeline topical analysis. This four-sequence exchange is useful because it also includes 'adjacency pairs', a concept developed by Schegloff and Sacks (1973, p. 296) to refer to a sequence of two utterances that follow each other, such as question-answer and invitation-acceptance.

The four-sequence exchange of Timeline topical analysis is applicable only to recent conversations on the Timeline. After a month, the latest four Comments are no longer displayed by default. Facebook sets all Comments to be hidden every time a new calendar month starts. At this point, the Friends who want to leave Comments will see only three links, which are Like, Comment and Share, as well as the Facebook name of the Friends who gave the latest two Likes (see Figure 1.3a). When the Comment link is clicked on by the Friend, only the Comment bar is displayed; therefore, to go through what has been said about the Status update, the Friend needs to click the 'View all x comments' link (see Figure 1.3b).

In the case of the non-recent Comment, it might be misleading to report that a Comment left by a Friend attempts to perform any topical action related to the earlier Comments because there is no way of knowing whether the Friend clicked the 'View all x comments' link to read through what had been written so far. Without clicking the link, the Friend is engaging in a dyadic conversation with the first topic introducer, the Profile owner who updated the Status. That is, it is a two-sequence exchange that takes place whereby the Comment performs a topical action in relation to the Status

(a)

(b)

Figure 1.3 Hidden non-recent Comments on Timelines

update, not the previous Comments. Because it is impossible to know whether the Friend clicked the 'View all x comments' link, any Comment not left in the same month as the Status update should not be included in the four-sequence exchange of Timeline topical analysis. Thus, only Comments posted in the same month as the Status update need to be taken into consideration so that the misrepresentation of data can be avoided.

Some of the extracts presented in this book are translated from Malay language because even though the research participants are English language teachers, they do not always update Statuses and post Comments in English. Forty-seven per cent ($n = 572$) of the Comments were written in a mixture of English and Malay. The code-switching can be seen as a discursive strategy to attract more supportive Comments, as it is likely that the topic will be continued by teaching Friends as well as non-teaching Friends with limited English proficiency. Only 19 per cent of the Comments were written in English and 34 per cent ($n = 418$) were written in Malay. The translated extracts are indicated in the source line, such as (Sharifa/SU8, translation by the author). Nonetheless, if the statements from the original sources are in comprehensible English, despite any grammatical errors, we attempt to avoid rephrasing them.

In the following chapters, the topical actions observed on teachers' Timelines as they co-construct social support are scrutinized to highlight the characteristics of each action.

References

Beaudin, B.P. (1999) Keeping online asynchronous discussions on topic. *Journal of Asynchronous Learning Network* [online] 3(2): pp. 41–53. Available at: http://myweb.fsu.edu/ajeong/eme5457/readings/Beaudin1999_KeepingOnTopic.pdf [Accessed 13 May 2013].

Brown, G. and Yule, G. (1983) *Discourse analysis*. Cambridge: Cambridge University Press.

Bublitz, W. (1988) *Supportive fellow-speakers and cooperative conversations*. Amsterdam: John Benjamins.

Coyle, A. (2006) Discourse analysis. In: Breakwell, G., Hammond, S., Fife-Schaw, C. and Smith, J. (Eds.) *Research methods in psychology*, pp. 366–387. Thousand Oaks, CA: Sage.

Gardner, R. (1987) The identification and role of topic in spoken interaction. *Semiotica* 65(1/2): pp. 129–141.

Keenan, E.O. and Schieffelin, B.B. (1976) Topic as a discourse notion: a study of topic in the conversations of children and adults. In: Li, C.N. (Ed.) *Subject and topic*, pp. 335–384. New York: Academic Press.

Rashid, R.A. (2016) Topic continuation strategies employed by teachers in managing supportive conversations on Facebook Timeline. *Discourse Studies* 18(2): pp. 188–203.

Sacks, H., Schegloff, E.A. and Jefferson, G. (1974) A simplest systematics for the organization of turn-taking for conversation. *Language* 50(4): pp. 696–735.

Schegloff, E.A. (1972) Notes on a conversational practice: formulating place. In: Sudnow, D. (Ed.) *Studies in social interaction*, pp. 75–119. New York: Free Press.

Schegloff, E.A. and Sacks, H. (1973) Opening up closing. *Semiotica* 7: pp. 289–327.

Sinclair, J.M. and Coulthard, M. (1975) *Towards an analysis of discourse: the English used by teachers and pupils*. London: Oxford University Press.

Sinclair, J.M. and Coulthard, M. (1992) Towards an analysis of discourse. In: Coulthard, M. (Ed.) *Advances in spoken discourse analysis*, pp. 1–34. London: Routledge.

Zitzen, M. (2004) *Topic shift markers in asynchronous and synchronous computer mediated communication (CMC)*. PhD Dissertation. Düsseldorf: University of Düsseldorf.

Zubiaga, A., Spina, D. and Martínez, R. (2011) Classifying trending topics: a typology of conversation triggers on Twitter. *20th ACM Conference proceedings* [online]. Available at: http://nlp.uned.es/~damiano/pdf/zubiaga2011trendingtopics. pdf [Accessed 19 January 2014].

2 Introducing a topic

Sample analysis of introducing a topic

There are three typical occasions when a speaker engages in the act of introducing the topic in everyday conversation (Bublitz, 1988). The first is at the beginning of the conversation. Usually, the first topic is introduced after the speaker deals with preliminary (phatic) actions, such as inquiring about health, offering a drink, complimenting clothes, and so forth. The second is during the course of the conversation if the speaker changes the topic by closing the current topic and introducing a new one. The third occasion is after a digression when the speaker reintroduces the topic after some kind of disturbance or interruption.

To introduce a particular topic, the speaker needs to highlight the 'subject' (Bublitz, 1988, p. 25) or what Schegloff and Sacks (1973, p. 301) label as 'mentionables', something that can grab other participants' attention. The participants might develop one of the subjects to become a topic subject and leave the remainder as undeveloped speech subjects. The mentionables or subjects can be divided into two types, 'personal' and 'impersonal' (Svennevig, 1999, p. 218). Personal mentionables are self-oriented, other-oriented or we-oriented and may involve 'past experiences, future plans [and the] personal characteristics' of selected individuals (p. 218). These personal mentionables may lead to the development of the three kinds of topics highlighted by Bublitz (1988) concerning the hearer (e.g. Do you like this work here?), the speaker (e.g. I'm applying for a job in Newcastle) or neither the hearer nor the speaker (e.g. Jane's away, isn't she?). On the other hand, impersonal mentionables involve the setting of the conversation and the participants' knowledge as members of a culture, such as 'media events, politics, literature, and music' (Svennevig, 1999, p. 218).

Speakers may employ either of two distinctive strategies to introduce a particular topic: 'itemized news inquiries' and 'news announcements' (Button and Casey, 1985, p. 4). Similar to other kinds of actions with an interrogative mood, itemized news inquiries postulate a gap in knowledge between speakers and recipients. The speaker makes two inferences by inquiring: that the specified item is newsworthy and that it is known about by the recipient.

News announcements, by contrast, are marked by the declarative mood and construct the topic introducer as more knowledgeable of the topic than the recipients. Nonetheless, the topic introducer provides only limited access to the matter raised and waits for the news recipients to feed back encouragement for the news to be fully revealed. Given the characteristic of the news announcement to reveal only partial information about the news, Button and Casey label the news announcement a 'headline' (p. 23). The news announcement might provoke announcement responses, elaboration of the news and then assessment of the news (Maynard, 2003), which might be part of the action of continuing the topic, the focus of the next chapter. The alternative strategies for introducing the topic are summarized in Figure 2.1.

Sample analysis of introducing a topic

Introducing the first topic of conversation on Timelines occurs when teachers update their Statuses. After this, Friends usually leave Comments and enable the topic to be continued, changed, digressed from, shifted or closed. This section discusses the two major forms of topic introduction and the rare cases of less successful and complete failure to introduce topics.

Two forms of topic introduction: news announcements and news inquiries

Teachers introduce a new topic to initiate a conversation either by reporting or by inquiring about something. The former is marked by the declarative mood, whereas the latter is marked by the interrogative mood. Sentence mood, in a general sense, is the way speakers express their attitude to what they say. These findings show that attempts to introduce a new topic on Timelines are similar to the attempts to introduce a topic in face-to-face conversation, where Button and Casey (1985, p. 4) put forth the concept that speakers in face-to-face conversation engage in 'news announcements' and 'itemized news inquiries' when nominating a topic. Given this similarity, the terms *news announcements* and *itemized news inquiries* are borrowed to use as a starting point to explain the action of introducing topics on Timelines.

The first form of topic introduction: the news announcement

News announcements report an activity (Button and Casey, 1985). Unlike itemized news inquiries that are marked with the interrogative mood, news announcements are marked with the declarative mood. On the Timelines, news announcements very much outnumber news inquiries. One possible

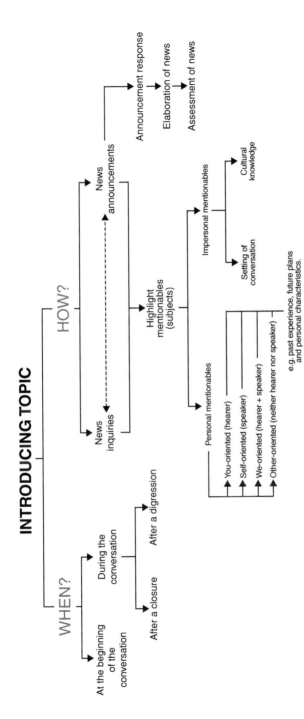

Figure 2.1 Analytical map of topic introduction

Source: Based on the synthesis of Schegloff and Sacks (1973), Button and Casey (1985), Bublitz (1988), Svennevig (1999), and Maynard (2003).

reason to explain this phenomenon is that Timelines share a similarity with personal diaries. Users record many things on Timelines, including their daily activities, their thoughts, their observations and their experiences (Page, 2010). In recording these moments, users recount what has happened to them, what they have in their minds and what they observe, rather than posing questions, as diaries and Timelines are not fellow humans with the capacity to answer questions. However, many people do write rhetorical or reflective questions in diaries.

However, unlike traditional diaries that are generally kept secret from others, Timelines make all the recorded moments visible to Friends or to the public, as users choose. Therefore, it is not surprising that the majority of Status updates take the form of news announcements, as the functionality of the Status update itself is designed so that users can share their news. Because Status updates are made accessible to Friends, there is a high possibility that the Friends will leave feedback, even though the Status updates do not take the form of news inquiries. At present, there are two triggers set by Facebook for Status updates: 'What's on your mind?' and 'What are you doing?' These kinds of questions encourage users to update Statuses in the form of news announcements rather than news inquiries.

Extract 2.1 scrutinizes an example of an attempt to introduce a topic that centres on a teacher's achievement. Sharifah introduced the topic by highlighting her successful classroom management strategy for students she considers to be problematic. To use a term from Button and Casey (1985), Sharifah 'announces' this news. This topic belongs to the second category of Bublitz's categorization of topic introduction in that it concerns the speaker and is 'self-oriented' Svennevig (1999, p. 218). This is discernible from the phrase *This is my way* (line 1) and the use of the personal pronoun *I* throughout the Status update.

Extract 2.1

1   This is my way:
2   Came to class teaching – class was noisy – I said please keep quiet –
3   class was noisy talking – I greeted them – they answered me – straight away I asked them to stand up and said nicely
4   "I allow you to sit down, you keep talking and ignore my lesson. Now I ask you to stand up, hopefully you will follow my lesson. If you are still noisy, you will stand on the chair till the end of the day"
5   Note: #my class flew smoothly for 1 hour 30 minutes
6   Next time I come to class, class is noisy, I just said
7   "ehem! Seems noisy! Don't want to sit perhaps" . . .

8   God willing, they will keep quiet, and learning process flows
     smoothly, hopefully . . .
9   Sometimes, even by being cool we still can control students . . .
     hehehe . . .

(Sharifah/SU3, translation by the author)

Using the pronoun *I*, Sharifah seems to take a pre-emptive step to avoid
disagreement, which might occur when Friends continue the topic. She
emphasizes that this is her way and that it works in her context. Therefore,
when continuing the topic, Friends or any other readers are not supposed
to criticize her if they disagree or do not like this strategy. However, by initiating this topic on her Timeline, it is reasonable to suggest that she seeks
social support in the form of praise from Friends, as she has discovered an
effective way to manage students. She believes that her newly discovered
strategy will also work for her Friends, and this is reflected through the
change of 'footing' (Goffman, 1983, p. 128) that is from *I* (lines 2, 3, 6) to
we (line 9). Hence, it is reasonable to suggest that what she expects from
Friends who want to develop this topic is to confirm that this kind of strategy also works for them by sharing their experiences and not challenging
or criticizing this strategy, as she concludes that *even by being cool* teachers still can control students (line 9). This is because any Comment condemning this strategy would tarnish her self-image as an effective teacher.
However, to avoid sounding as though she is persuading Friends to employ
this strategy, or perhaps not to sound too proud of her own achievement in
handling the problematic students, Sharifah ends this Status update with
laughter *hehehe* (line 9), which makes the conclusion placed before this
laughter sound more like a joke.

Introducing topics in the form of a news announcement, especially in
the Status updates that centre on teachers' achievements, may benefit the
teacher community on Facebook because it offers an opportunity for teachers to learn how to improve their teaching efficiency by engaging in vicarious learning. As pointed out by Cox et al. (1999), the concept of vicarious
learning highlights 'the potential benefit to learners of being able to observe
or "listen in" on experts or their peers as they discuss a new topic' (p. 432).
In this case, the Friends may learn from the successful experience shared by
Sharifah. It is in this sense that Timelines may be a good platform to engage
teachers in informal learning.

Extract 2.2 examines an example of topic introduction where teachers
'announce' their feelings with regards to educational policy. In this Status update, Syiba introduces the topic by highlighting the unintended con-
sequences that might arise when the government allows students to bring

mobile phones into school. This topic is categorized as 'other-oriented' (Svennevig, 1999, p. 218) in that it concerns neither the speaker nor the hearer directly, which is the third category of Bublitz's (1988) categorization of topic introductions. This is because it concerns an educational policy that relates to students and not directly to teachers.

Extract 2.2

1 so the government wants to allow students to bring mobile phones to school next year . . .
2 believe me beb, I'm a teacher, used 2 b a warden . . .
3 don't regret if many students elope with men on the way going to / returning from school . . .
4 many cases already happened . . .

(Syiba/SU11, translation by the author)

Syiba begins this Status update with the discourse marker *so* to draw readers' attention to the specific policy that she refers to, allowing *students to bring mobile phones to school* (line 1). Discourse markers are words or phrases, such as *anyway*, *right* and *okay*, that are used to connect, organize and manage discourse or to express attitude (Müller, 2005). Syiba then starts to give her opinion regarding the policy so that her topic introduction is easy for readers to follow. It is discernible that she has a negative opinion or disagrees with this policy when she highlights the possible consequence that many more female students will *elope with men* (line 3). In giving this opinion, Syiba does not simply give an opinion but justifies it from her experience of being *a warden* (line 2) in that she knows many problems have arisen when students have brought mobile phones to school (line 4).

Even though Syiba does not agree with the educational policy, she is careful not to condemn it. As can be seen in the Status update, she does not directly criticize the policy by condemning its rationale, but she draws her Friends' attention towards the unintended consequences that might arise. Hence, Syiba seems to initiate a conversation to evaluate the pros and cons of implementing this policy. Yet her stance is clearly indicated that she believes this policy might lead to an increase in elopements, and the phrase *believe me* (line 2) suggests that she is persuading Friends to support this stance. Receiving Comments that support the stance is important to Syiba, as this will make her feel emotionally supported by like-minded Friends.

When introducing topics in the form of news announcements, teachers not only share their negative feelings regarding particular aspects of their professional lives (e.g. the implementation of educational policy) but also promote their achievements. This suggests that Status updates are a mechanism for teachers to seek social support and to construct their desired self-images.

The second form of topic introduction: itemized news inquiries

Itemized news inquiries aim to direct a conversation to a particular item (Button and Casey, 1985) in parallel to the action of inquiring about something specific observed on a Timeline, as shown in Extract 2.3. From the perspective of social support put forth by Beehr and Glazer (2001), itemized news inquiries can be seen as an attempt to seek informational support.

Extract 2.3

1   Anyone involved with the English drama competition for johor bahru district???
2   when and where will it be held?

(Fazry/SU1)

Fazry introduces the topic to find out the latest news about an educational activity, seeking informational support. He asks whether any of his Friends know the time and venue for the English drama competition at Johor Bahru district level. This finding is in line with the purpose of itemized news inquiries in everyday face-to-face conversation (Button and Casey, 1985), where a topic introducer may ask to be brought up to date with the latest news about an activity or circumstance.

The topic introduced by Fazry is 'other-oriented' (Svennevig, 1999, p. 218) and belongs to the third category of Bublitz's (1988) categorization of topic introduction in that it concerns neither the speaker nor the hearer directly. The topic subject in this Status update is *English drama competition* (line 1), and there is not enough information to say that this topic concerns Fazry. He might have introduced it because he is involved with the drama competition, or he might be asking on behalf of someone else. However, he introduces the topic to seek information, which suggests that interactions that occur on Facebook may make a significant contribution to teachers' professional lives.

Besides the news inquiry relating to the seeking of practical information, there are also Status updates in the form of news inquiries seeking Friends' personal opinions regarding particular problematic aspects of teachers' professional lives. In Extract 2.4, Barnett introduces a topic by asking for her Friends' opinions about whether it is fair to Unfriend all her current students on Facebook. This topic is 'self-oriented' (Svennevig, 1999, p. 218) and relates to the second category of Bublitz's (1988) categorization of topic introduction in that it concerns the speaker, specifically about what Button and Casey (1985) refer to as the speaker's trouble. The trouble is that Barnett feels that she is losing her privacy on Facebook. It is interesting that Barnett talks about the students whom she approved as Friends. This provides the opportunity for the students to contribute to this Timeline discussion, perhaps by apologizing or defending themselves.

Extract 2.4

1   Is it fair to unfriend all the current students on FB?
2   I feel like I have no privacy anymore

(Barnett/SU19)

The 'self-orientedness' of this topic is discernible from line 2, where Barnet uses the personal pronoun *I* in giving the reason that motivates her to Unfriend her current students, indicating that this topic is about her and the loss of her privacy. By introducing this topic, Barnett seems to hope that Friends will develop it further by giving their opinions on whether to Unfriend the students.

To encourage Friends to take up this topic, Barnett gives a piece of background information in line 2. To some extent, it can be inferred that Barnett is hoping Friends will leave Comments encouraging her to Unfriend the students, as she highlights a strong reason for her to Unfriend them, which is the potential violation of her privacy. Therefore, this topic, even though marked with an interrogative mood, should not be seen as a genuine inquiry about the fairness to Unfriend current students on Facebook but rather as an attempt to seek social support from Friends to avoid feeling guilty when unfriending all her current students on Facebook.

Extract 2.5 is an example of how teachers introduce topics in the form of a news inquiry for them to challenge or deconstruct the views they do not agree with.

Extract 2.5

1   Malaysian English language teachers need to improve English up to BBC standard,
2   but MOE [Ministry of Education] is importing English language teachers from USA??
3   so confusing . . .

(Sharifah/SU8, translation by the author)

Sharifah introduces the topic by questioning the rationale behind the MoE's decision to import English language teachers from the United States. To justify her question, she reveals her perception that Malaysian English language teachers are expected to use British English (line 1). This topic is categorized as 'other-oriented' (Svennevig, 1999, p. 218) because even though the topic subject is about the MoE's decision, which relates to Sharifah and her Friends who are English language teachers, it is neither made personal (as that of Barnett in Extract 2.4) nor is it specifically addressed to any officer from the MoE.

Even though Sharifah seems to make an itemized news inquiry with question marks in line 2, it is hard to conclude that she introduces the topic to fill a knowledge vacuum or gap to share information regarding the latest development in educational policy. It is more reasonable to conclude that she introduces the topic to show her disagreement with the MoE's decision and to seek support. This is strongly supported by the phrase *so confusing* (line 3), which suggests that she sees an inconsistency in the educational policy. Hence, it can be inferred that by introducing this topic, she does not expect her Friends to take it up by giving factual information – for example, relating to teachers from the United States. She hopes her Friends will give their opinions on whether it is a wise decision to import teachers from the United States whilst at the same time requiring local teachers to use *BBC standard* (line 1).

Sharifah introduces the topic by criticizing and explicitly showing her disagreement with the topic subject. This reflects her readiness to argue with Friends who might agree with the MoE's decision and thus have conflicting views to hers. Given that this Status update is set to be seen by all Friends, she can be considered brave enough to indicate her stance regarding this particular issue. She could have chosen to introduce the topic in a safer way that would make her sound more neutral, such as 'I wonder why the MoE has decided to import English language teachers from the USA when Malaysian English language teachers are required to use BBC standard English', but she chooses not to. Her disagreement is made explicit by having double question marks in line 2 and the phrase *so confusing* in line 3.

One possible reason why teachers have the courage to explicitly indicate their disagreement or stance regarding particular issues, especially regarding educational policies, is because they believe their Friends have similar opinions regarding those issues and are supportive towards them. When connecting with like-minded people, teachers are unlikely to attract objections or disagreements when they indicate a particular stance. Timelines have become a platform for teachers to highlight their own stances on particular issues without having to fear rejection and objections from others. Having the opportunity to talk about their own stance without fear of rejection is crucial for teacher professional development, especially in the Malaysian context, as according to Mukundan and Khandehroo (2010), many Malaysian English language teachers suffer from burnout due to the suppression of their views in their working environment.

Despite some similarities in the ways teachers introduce topics on Timelines, there is one characteristic of topic introduction in face-to-face conversation as listed by Button and Casey (1985) that is not found on Facebook: 'the solicitous inquiries into troubles which recipients are known to have' (p. 8). One possible reason is that inquiring about Friends' troubles openly on their Timelines might embarrass them; thus, teachers avoid engaging in such actions. This suggests that teachers are careful not to tarnish their Friends' self-images in an online environment like Facebook by initiating talk about their troubles. However, there are occasions when teachers talk about their own troubles in the topic, such as in Extract 2.4, where Barnett shares her trouble, which is the violation of privacy by her students. When teachers choose to make their own troubles the topic of conversation, it is often to seek advice from Friends. Solicitous inquiries into Friends' troubles might occur in Private Messages and are therefore outside the scope of this study.

Teachers introduce topics in the form of news inquiries to serve three different purposes. All three purposes identified support the argument that Timeline postings are used as a mechanism for teachers to seek social support, as indicated,

1   to find information, such as the details of curricular activities (informational support);
2   to gather Friends' opinions regarding particular troubles in their professional lives (emotional support – advice); and
3   to challenge or deconstruct teaching-related views they do not agree with (emotional support – solidarity).

Data analysis shows that topics introduced are often taken up by Friends (see Chapter 3), which indicates the strong presence of structural support on Timelines. Structural support is associated with the existence of supportive others (Beehr and Glazer, 2001) – in this case, the supportive Friends on the site. Nonetheless, there are a few rare cases of unsuccessful attempts to introduce topics, which will be discussed in the next subsection.

Less successful/unsuccessful attempts at introducing a topic

Even though Status updates usually attract Comments, there are occasions when they are ignored by Friends and no topical action follows the attempt to introduce a topic. For an event, a state, an action or a person to be made a topic subject, there must be 'something interesting, worth knowing and possibly new and unforeseen to say about them' (Bublitz, 1988, pp. 46–47). The ability to delete an unsuccessful topic is unique to conversations that occur on a social media platform like Facebook. In daily face-to-face conversation, speakers cannot 'unsay' what they have said, and so their options are either to continue promoting the topic or to give in and take up a new topic introduced by another speaker. As Facebook enables the deletion of the topic and the replacing of it with a new one, users do not have to give in to take up a new topic introduced by Friends but instead have endless opportunities to experiment with the topic introduction to find the kind of topic that will yield responses from Friends.

In addition to completely unsuccessful attempts at introducing a topic, there is another phenomenon that can be considered only a partially successful attempt at topic introduction. This occurs when teachers update their Statuses and receive no Comments, only Likes, indicating that the audience likes the topic or agrees with the issue or opinion brought up but makes no attempt at topical actions to continue or further expand the topic. Teachers seem to be able to tolerate less successful attempts at introducing a topic in the sense that they usually do not delete the Status updates that receive Like(s). Perhaps this is because they feel they have received positive responses from Friends.

References

Beehr, T. and Glazer, S. (2001) A cultural perspective of social support in relation to occupational stress. In: Perrewe, P., Ganster, D.C. and Moran, J. (Eds.) *Research in occupational stress and wellbeing*, pp. 97–142. Greenwich, CO: JAI Press.

Bublitz, W. (1988) *Supportive fellow-speakers and cooperative conversations*. Amsterdam: John Benjamins.

Button, G. and Casey, N. (1985) Topic nomination and topic pursuit. *Human Studies* [online] 8(3): pp. 3–55. Available at: http://dx.doi.org/10.1007%2fBF00143022 [Accessed 6 May 2016].

Cox, R., McKendree, J., Tobin, R., Lee, J. and Mayes, T. (1999) Vicarious learning from dialogue and discourse: a controlled comparison. *Instructional Science* [online] 27: pp. 431–458. Available at: http://dx.doi.org/10.1023/A:1003489631631 [Accessed 2 January 2015].

Goffman, E. (1983) Felicity's condition. *American Journal of Sociology* 89(1): pp. 1–53.

Maynard, D.W. (2003) *Bad news good news: conversational order in everyday talk and clinical settings*. Chicago: University of Chicago Press.

Mukundan, J. and Khandehroo, K. (2010) Burnout among English language teachers in Malaysia. *Contemporary Issues in Education Research* 3(1): pp. 71–76.

Müller, S. (2005) *Discourse markers in native and non-native English*. Amsterdam: John Benjamins.

Page, R. (2010) Re-examining narrativity: small stories in Status updates. *Text & Talk: An Interdisciplinary Journal of Language, Discourse & Communication Studies* [online] 30(4): pp. 423–444. Available at: http://dx.doi.org/10.1515/text.2010.021 [Accessed 11 May 2013].

Schegloff, E.A. and Sacks, H. (1973) Opening up closing. *Semiotica* 7: pp. 289–327.

Svennevig, J. (1999) *Getting acquainted in conversation: a study of initial interactions*. Amsterdam: John Benjamins.

3 Continuing a topic

Sample analysis of continuing a topic

A topic is continued when the 'primary presupposition in an exchange is linked directly to the primary presupposition entailed in the utterances of the immediately preceding exchange' (Gardner, 1987, p. 138). Continuing a topic requires the cooperation of the participants, as it needs to be taken up by others after it has been introduced. This can be done by 'establishing local links and producing informative, coherent contributions' (Svennevig, 1999, p. 173). If nobody comments on the topic subject, the topic will come to a halt. A topic may be continued not only because the speakers are interested in the content but also for them to provide other information, such as their desired self-image and certain impressions of their 'ideas, principles, tendencies, opinion and attitudes' (Bublitz, 1988, p. 84). A typical example of topic continuation is when listeners comment on and respond to the telling of a story (Gardner, 1987).

Sacks, Schegloff and Jefferson (1974), Maynard (1980) and West and Garcia (1988) all agree that the action of continuing a topic can be determined only by examining the turn-taking that takes place in the conversation because the topic 'can hardly be confirmed into existence until it is taken up in a series of subsequent utterances' (Goffman, 1983, p. 11). In other words, it is the turns following the topic introduction that will show whether the topic has been accepted and continued or rejected by the recipients.

Drawing on Button and Casey (1984), Svennevig (1999), Radford and Tarplee (2000) and Sukrutrit (2010), Jeon (2012) suggests four possible ways for recipients to engage in continuing a topic. To begin with, the recipients may produce 'topicalisers' (Jeon, 2012, p. 153), which are utterances that indicate their interest in taking up the topic. The most common topicalisers in British English are *Really?*, *Oh yeah?* and *Oh really?*, which reflect feelings of surprise and signal that the topic subject is newsworthy. Besides producing topicalisers, participants may also give Schegloff and Sacks' (1973, p. 295) 'preferred responses', such as positive answers to questions posed by the topic introducer, or any minimal positive responses, such as *uh-huh, um-hmm, mm* and *hmm.* Producing topicalisers and pre-ferred responses are closely related to each other in the sense that partici-pants' interests in taking up the topic are made clear. Consequently, the topic introducer will further elaborate the topic subject, as receiving the preferred responses suggests that the recipients are interested (Schegloff, 2007) and being attentive (Abu-Akel, 2002) as well as understanding the aboutness of the topic (Maynard, 1980).

The third way of continuing a topic, highlighted by Jeon (2012), is by repeating part of the topic introducer's turn or using appropriate deictic rearrangement, such as *it, this* and *that.* Similar to the function of topi-calisers and preferred responses, repeating part(s) of the topic introducer's talk suggests the recipients are interested in continuing the topic. Last but not least, the participants may ask questions if they want to continue the topic. Unlike topicalisers, which can also take the form of an inquiry (e.g. *Really?*), asking questions to continue the topic can be a genuine inquiry to gain clarification or more information about the topic subject. Gardner (1987, p. 138) highlights two possible questions for these purposes – *Could you explain that again?* and *What happened next?*

Whether a topic is continued depends very much on the participants' interest in the topic subject. A topic introducer needs to be able to recognize when the other participants (hearers/recipients) are interested in taking up the topic in order to further elaborate the topic subject. This is because dis-couraging responses, such as receiving the news with *Oh* (Maynard, 2003), may stop the topic introducer from further commenting on the topic, so the topic will be closed and a new topic introduced. The topical action of con-tinuing the topic is summarized in Figure 3.1.

Sample analysis of continuing a topic

Continuing the first topic can be said to take place when the Comments left by Friends following the Status updated by the Profile owner can be 'linked directly' (Gardner, 1987, p. 138) to the Status update. There are four possible ways for the participants to continue the topic, which Jeon (2012) argues are relevant to both online and offline settings: (1) producing 'topi-calisers' (p. 153), (2) giving Schegloff and Sacks' (1973, p. 295) 'preferred responses', (3) repeating some parts of the topic introducer's talk, and (4) asking questions for further elaboration on the topic. A close examination of the Comments reveals that all four possible ways of continuing the topic are employed by teachers. We did not identify any additional strategies, which suggests that strategies for continuing the topic on Timelines are sim-ilar to strategies for continuing the topic in an offline setting. In this section, we scrutinize the action of continuing the topic, which we argue reflects the

CONTINUING TOPIC

WHEN?
- When the introduced topic is taken up (e.g. listeners respond to the telling of the story).

WHY?
- Participants are interested in the topic
- Construct desired self-image/particular impression

HOW?
- Establish local links
- Produce informative/coherent contributions
- Give preferred responses (e.g. positive answer or positive minimal responses)
- Produce topicalisers (e.g. Really?)
- Repeat some parts of topic introducer's talk
- Ask questions for further elaboration (e.g. What happened next?)

Figure 3.1 Analytical map of topic continuation

Source: Based on the synthesis of Schegloff and Sacks (1973), Button and Casey (1984), Gardner (1987), Bublitz (1988), Svennevig (1999), Radford and Tarplee (2000), Abu-Akel (2002), Schegloff (2007), Sukrutrit (2010), and Jeon (2012).

strong presence of structural support on Facebook in the sense that Friends show their interest in co-constructing social support by taking up the topic.

Following Barnett's Status update where she introduced the first topic by expressing her anger towards students who she thinks are spoilt, rude and not learning anything after being taught for almost a year, four Comments were left on the Timeline, of which three are from Friends and one is from Barnett herself. The Comments are presented in Extract 3.1.

Extract 3.1

1	Sue:	Be patient . . . that's the challenge . . . huhu
2	Zura:	So heart wrenching, isn't it? hurmm
3	Piya:	Be patient . . . thinking about it really painful . . . but what to do . . . need to recite Quranic verse before you enter the class
4	Barnett:	Quranic verses are read every day during the assembly.
5		Even on entering the class, we read prayer to enlighten the heart. But they are really stubborn.
6		No effect at all.

(Barnett/SU22/C1-4, translation by the author)

Because Barnett expresses anger in the Status update, Sue can be said to engage in the act of giving a preferred response when she leaves the first Comment advising Barnett to be patient and tries to comfort Barnett with the phrase *that's the challenge* (line 1). Sue ends her line with *huhu* (line 1), which can be associated with the feeling of sympathy, suggesting that she was not attempting to play the role of an expert when she advised Barnett but more of an empathetic colleague.

Zura, who posted a Comment after Sue, does not shift the topic to talk about *challenge* (line 1) but still deals directly with the first topic by producing the topicaliser, *So heart wrenching, isn't it?* (line 2). Even though there is a question mark in Zura's line, it cannot be seen as a genuine act of questioning. It is more reasonable to see this line as performing the function of a topicaliser, which encourages Barnett to further express her feelings and to vent her anger. Zura ends her line with *hurmm* (line 2), which indicates that she is also not happy with how Barnett's students behave, hence signalling to Barnett that her anger is justified.

Piya, who leaves the third Comment, also makes no attempt to interact with the Friends who left the previous Comments. She does not take up any subject from Sue or Zura (e.g. *challenge* or *heart wrenching*) but instead relates her Comment directly to Barnett's Status update. When Piya advised Barnett to *be patient* (line 3), the same advice given by Sue, she is not developing Sue's advice. It is just a piece of similar advice that comes from her and is addressed directly to Barnett. This is because if she attempts to develop *be patient* as a topic subject, she would say, 'agree with Sue, we need to be patient', or rather more implicitly, 'yeah, be patient', which would indicate a link between the two Comments. Even though Sue and Piya give similar preferred responses to Barnett by attempting to calm her down, Piya goes a bit further by suggesting what Barnett could do in future to lessen the problem.

From Barnett's Comment (lines 4–6), it is clear that Piya has success-fully elicited a response from Barnett about the topic. Barnett seems to ignore Sue and Zura's Comments but responds to Piya's suggestion for her to recite Quranic verse, where she claims that reading Quranic verse and prayer have *no effect at all* (line 6) because the students are *really stubborn* (line 5). One possible reason for Barnett to focus her Comment on Piya's suggestion is because Piya seems to blame Barnett for the students' misbe-haviour in that she does not read enough prayer and Quranic verses before she enters the classroom. Thus, when Barnett emphasizes that she reads Quranic verses and prayers with the class *every day* (line 4), her response could be seen as an attempt to protect her 'face', which is her positive self-image (Brown and Levinson,1987). Barnett's reaction, as shown in this extract, confirms the finding reported by Bublitz (1988) that a topic is con-tinued not only because the participants are interested in the content but also for them to construct the desired self-image and manage a particular impression.

Analysis of Extract 3.1, which is an example of the typical type of con-versation that occurs on Timelines, reveals some interesting characteristics of this new mode of online interaction. Firstly, even though the conversa-tion seems to involve a group of Friends (e.g. Sue, Zura, Piya and Barnett) and Barnett receives 'multiparty feedback' (Copland, 2012, p. 2), it actu-ally takes the dyadic form of conversation; it is a series of conversations between two people: Sue and Barnett, Zura and Barnett, and Piya and Bar-nett. This multiple dyadic conversation contributes to the continuation of the topic as the topic introducer senses the interest of the topic from every Friend in this set of dyadic conversations, hence developing an awareness that the topic is newsworthy.

The second characteristic relates to the strategy of encouraging the topic introducer to talk more about the topic. Multiple strategies are used to encourage Barnett to elaborate on the topic, such as giving preferred responses (e.g. Sue) and producing topicalisers (e.g. Zura). The more the topic introducer postpones his or her reply, the more strategies might be employed by the Friends to elicit the topic introducer's response. In a face-to-face conversation, silence from the speaker after elicitation attempts by other speakers might make them stop attempting to elicit further comment, as silence may signal unwillingness to talk. However, in an asynchronous Timeline conversation, Friends might associate delayed responses with the asynchronous nature of the platform; hence, it may not stop them from continuing to elicit the topic introducer's responses. This implies that the extended 'wait-time', which is the delay between an initiation and a response (Walsh, 2006, p. 134), might increase the number of Comments, hence opening up more opportunities for different topical actions to be performed.

The third characteristic is that the topic introducer holds the power about whom he or she wants to respond to. Barnett chose to respond only to Piya and ignored Sue and Zura. In this case, Barnett can do this without having to feel guilty because she does not specifically 'invite' any Friends using the tagging function to join the conversation. Friends join conversations on a voluntary basis and hence she has no obligation to respond to all the Comments.

Another example of how a topic is continued through giving preferred responses is shown in Extract 3.2. Prior to these Comments, Wafi introduces the topic by presenting two identical sentences and asks her Friends which sentence is grammatically correct. This topic attracted 18 Comments, three times higher than the average number of Comments received by a Status update, which is six to seven Comments. The high number of Comments received by Status updates on teaching-related knowledge suggests that teachers do not only engage in the co-construction of emotional support but also in teaching-related informational resources, which could be seen as attempts to engage in informal learning. In Extract 3.2, the first four-sequence exchange is presented to examine the topic continuation.

Extract 3.2

1	Wafi:	*Barnett, Amin, Ida*
2	Tan:	Dont hesitate, or Dont be hesitant
3	Tan:	Hesitate is a verb, so you dont have to add be in front
4	Barnett:	A is correct. B sounds strange . . .

(Wafi/SU2/C1-4)

Wafi leaves the first Comment following her own Status update. In this, she tags three Friends: Barnett, Amin and Ida. By doing this, Wafi sends an invitation to these Friends to contribute to the topic. Because she addresses this Status update to the *grammar nazi* on her Timeline, it suggests that she views these three Friends as more knowledgeable than herself about grammar.

Interestingly, it is not the tagged Friends who give the first responses to Barnet but another teaching Friend (Tan). Tan continues the topic by giving two preferred responses in two separate Comments. Tan's first Comment (line 2) provides an answer to Wafi's question, and her second Comment gives an explanation of the answer because in the Status update, Wafi does not only request an answer but also an explanation. It is not rare on Timelines for untagged Friend(s) to give quicker responses than tagged Friends. This implies that there is a high level of willingness for teachers to help one another, especially when it comes to teaching-related knowledge.

Barnett, one of the tagged Friends, gives her Comment only after Tan has convincingly answered Wafi's question. Although this delay might be due to lack of access to Facebook, another possible reason is because she needs to be really sure to give a correct answer. This is because she is one of those Friends presented as a *grammar nazi* by Wafi and giving the wrong answer might tarnish her ascribed identity. Barnett seems to agree with Tan that *hesitate* is correct (line 4), but her Comment has no direct link to Tan's Comment, indicating she is talking directly to Wafi, having a dyadic conversation. If she wanted to have a group conversation to include herself, Wafi and Tan, she would have linked her Comment to Tan's Comment, such as *yeah . . . A is correct*. In comparison to Tan, Barnett seems to be unable to give a convincing explanation, as she says only that *B sounds strange* (line 4). Notwithstanding that, Barnett's Comment does not contradict Tan's Comment, and it can be seen as reinforcement, hence enabling Wafi to internalize this new knowledge without having any doubts. This is an example of teachers' participation on Facebook providing an opportunity for them to engage in informal learning.

Despite several Comments left by different Friends following Wafi's Status update, there is no complex conversational pattern observable. All the Friends are more interested in having a dialogic interaction with the topic introducer (Wafi); hence, they do not talk to the other Friends. Thus, in a Status update that attracts many Comments, there will be many sets of dyadic conversations taking place. This phenomenon closely resembles what usually happens in a classroom where a teacher who is a 'power role holder' (O'Keeffe, McCarthy and Carter, 2007, p. 176) poses a question, and students answer one by one by talking to the teacher (not one another), commonly in an initiation-response-feedback pattern (Sinclair and Coulthard, 1975). It also resonates with Evison's (2013) finding that in academic discourse, interactions mainly occur between two persons, involving an expert (the teacher) and a novice (the student), where the expert is in charge of directing the conversation. This implies that topic introducers who are also Profile owners have the power to control the progress of topical actions on Timelines, as all the Comments are left as a direct response to them, and hence they can choose whose contribution they want to expand or halt.

Extract 3.3 is an example of how a topic is continued by using the strategy of repeating some parts of the topic introducer's words. Prior to the Comments shown in Extract 3.3, Zeti introduces the first topic by grumbling about the heavy workload that teachers have and praises them for their ability to cope with the workload and time pressures. There are 12 Comments altogether following the Status update, but only the first set of four-sequence exchange is presented here, as the last Comment in the exchange (line 4) is a move to shift the topic instead of continuing with the same topic. The action of shifting a topic is discussed in Chapter 6.

Extract 3.3

1   Ira: Online system is problematic. Moreover now SPPBS is temporarily closed. Haihhhhhhh
2   Zeti: often closed . . .
3   Ira: X stable yet perhaps . . .
4   Zeti: but when they give out instruction everything is urgent . . .

(Zeti/SU1/C1-4)

Ira repeats Zeti's suggestion that the online system is *problematic* (line 1), and she re-highlights the acronym of one of the online systems mentioned by Zeti in the Status update, *SPPBS*. Interestingly, she does not simply repeat the acronym but adds further information that the SPPBS *is temporarily closed* (line 1). By giving this information, Ira indicates that she agrees with the time pressure issue brought up by Zeti that teachers still cannot key in data despite the approaching deadline due to the system failure. The long sigh indicated by *Haihhhhhh* (line 1) reflects the intensity of the pressure faced by Ira. Ira's response to the Status update manages to encourage Zeti to talk more about the problem with the online system that it is *often closed* (line 2), suggesting that this is a recurring problem and thus heightening the severity of the time pressure issue. When Ira says that it is *not stable yet* (line 3), she seems to refer to some kind of rationalization of the problem. This line has positive connotations because it reflects Ira's optimistic perception that the system will get better with time, thus serving the function of comforting Zeti that the problem will stop one day and teachers' professional lives will finally get better. In line 4, Zeti attempts to shift the topic to talk about the problematic administrator whom she views as being non-realistic when giving instructions. Shifting the topic is discussed in Chapter 6.

The dyadic interaction involving only two people (e.g. between Zeti and Ira) shown in Extract 3.3 is another example of a common conversational pattern found on Timelines besides the multiple dyadic conversations highlighted in Extracts 3.1 and 3.2. The two conversational patterns identified so far are illustrated in Figure 3.2.

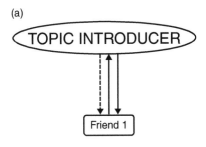

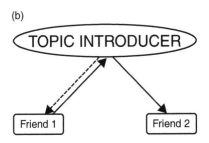

Figure 3.2 Single and multiple dyadic conversations on Timelines

Extract 3.4 examines how a topic is continued using the strategy of asking questions. The topic introduced prior to the Comments can be associated with the teachers' attempts to engage in informal learning on Timelines, where Jaya introduces the topic by asking her Friend Cheng Chong Hung (pseudonym) how to handle school-based assessment (SBA) for English as a subject in lower secondary schools.

Extract 3.4

1	Cheng Chong Hung:	Do you have to prepare your own SBA assessments?
2		Is there a standardized one in the school?
3	Jaya:	if am not mistaken there are a few publication such as pelangi . . . setiamas that my current sch are holding on to . . .
4		so just use that as worksheet . . . mark . . . n key in marks is it?
5		so wen is the nrml pnp like?
6		am confused *Cheng Chong Hung* . . . huhu

7	Cheng Chong Hung:	Pnp still carry on. But have to include SBA.
8		I am not sure about selangor, but in pasir gudang . . .
9		can't write in the record book that we did SBA.
10		Here, the minimum requirement is band one.
11		So for the end classes just help and guide them to achieve.
12		As for the good classes (with the potential to obtain band 6)
13		you really need to plan your lessons so that you can cover the syllabus and let students try band 6.
14	Cheng Chong Hung:	Try coordinating with other teachers teaching English in the same form.
15		Else coming out with your own SBA sheets is very taxing.
16		It should be done during the holidays.
17		Btw, cannot use published materials.
18		Cause students can get the answers by buying and it becomes invalid.

(Jaya/SU1/C1-4)

Cheng Chong Hung attempts to continue the topic by asking two questions in her first Comment (lines 1 and 2), suggesting that she has a high level of interest in the topic introduced and signalling to Jaya that she needs more information before she can provide appropriate feedback. The topic is continued when Jaya responds to Cheng Chong Hung's questions by listing the educational publishers, Pelangi and Setiamas, of books that her current school is holding on to regarding SBA assessment (line 3). To further develop the topic, Jaya poses two new questions about the implementation of SBA in lines 4 and 5. Jaya's first question is a closed question that requires only a yes-or-no answer, whilst the second question is more open, requiring some explanation from Cheng Chong Hung. Nonetheless, as can be seen from Cheng Chong Hung's second and third Comments, she gives elaborated responses to both questions. She not only provides answers to the two questions but also gives tips and guidance – for instance, on how to manage weak and advanced classes differently (lines 11–13), to coordinate with other teachers teaching English in the same form (line 14), to do SBA sheets during the holidays (line 16) and to avoid using published materials (line 17).

The elaborated responses from Cheng Chong Hung provide informational support to make sure that the *confused* (line 6) Jaya fully understands how to conduct SBA assessments in lower secondary school. Nonetheless, there is not enough information to conclude that learning has occurred, that Jaya has managed to understand what has been explained to her, as she provides no Comment following Cheng Chong Hung's final answer. Notwithstanding that, Jaya shows some attempt to engage in informal learning by inquiring about the SBA assessment, and Cheng Chong Hung is supportive of this by giving elaborated responses. This phenomenon is not uncommon on Timelines. Teachers' attempts to introduce a topic by inquiring about such 'teacher knowledge' (Shulman, 1987, p. 8) as 'content knowledge', 'pedagogical knowledge' and 'pedagogical-content knowledge' are rarely ignored by Friends, which reflects the potential of Timelines to be a supportive platform for teachers to engage in informal learning.

All the strategies for continuing topics listed by Jeon (2012) are creatively employed by teachers on Timelines. There are six characteristics of Timeline conversations that emerged from the analysis of topic continuation, which can be summarized as follows:

1   The delayed response from topic introducers encourages different Friends to employ different strategies in their attempts to ensure the continuation of the topic.
2   Most conversation takes the dyadic form, which involves only two people (a Friend and the topic introducer). Hence, a topic that attracts many Comments will produce multiple dyadic forms.
3   The topic introducer holds the power to designate whom she or he wants to respond to upon receiving Comments from different Friends.
4   When inquiring about teaching-related knowledge, the topic introducer tends to 'invite' specific Friends who they think are expert in the subject of inquiry by tagging their Facebook names.
5   Even though a topic introducer tags specific Friends to contribute to the continuation of a topic, other Friends who are not tagged can still join in the conversation, which reflects the high level of structural support on Facebook.
6   Interesting topics either attract many quick responses from Friends or elaborated responses from a few Friends.

References

Abu-Akel, A. (2002) The psychological and social dynamics of topic performance in family dinner time conversation. *Journal of Pragmatics* [online] 34(12): pp. 1787–1806. Available at: http://dx.doi.org/10.1016/S0378-2166(01)00054-6 [Accessed 10 March 2013].

Brown, P. and Levinson, S. (1987) *Politeness: some universals in language usage.* Cambridge: Cambridge University Press.

Bublitz, W. (1988) *Supportive fellow-speakers and cooperative conversations*. Amsterdam: John Benjamins.

Button, G. and Casey, N. (1984) Generating topic: the use of topic initial elicitors. In: Atkinson, J.M. and Heritage, J.C. (Eds.) *Structures of social action: studies in conversation analysis*, pp. 167–190. Cambridge: Cambridge University Press.

Copland, F. (2012) Legitimate talk in feedback conferences. *Applied Linguistics* [online] 33(1): pp. 1–20. Available at: http://dx.doi.org/10.1093/applin/amr040 [Accessed 7 May 2014].

Evison, J. (2013) Turn openings in academic talk: where goals and roles intersect. *Classroom Discourse* [online] 4(1): pp. 3–26. Available at: http://dx.doi.org/10.1 080/19463014.2013.783499 [Accessed 13 April 2014].

Gardner, R. (1987) The identification and role of topic in spoken interaction. *Semiotica* 65(1/2): pp. 129–141.

Goffman, E. (1983) Felicity's condition. *American Journal of Sociology* 89(1): pp. 1–53.

Jeon, S. (2012) *Management of topics in online one-to-one English conversation instruction: a micro-analytic investigation of computer-mediated communication*. PhD Thesis. Newcastle upon Tyne: Newcastle University.

Maynard, D.W. (1980) Placement of topic changes in conversation. *Semiotica* 30: pp. 263–290.

Maynard, D.W. (2003) *Bad news good news: conversational order in everyday talk and clinical settings*. Chicago: University of Chicago Press.

O'Keeffe, A., McCarthy, M. and Carter, R. (2007) *From corpus to classroom: language use and language teaching*. Cambridge: Cambridge University Press.

Radford, J. and Tarplee, C. (2000) The management of conversational topic by a 10-year old child with pragmatic difficulties. *Clinical Linguistics and Phonetics* [online] 14(5): pp. 387–403. Available at: http://dx.doi.org/10.1080/02699200050051092 [Accessed 20 May 2013].

Sacks, H., Schegloff, E.A. and Jefferson, G. (1974) A simplest systematics for the organization of turn-taking for conversation. *Language* 50(4): pp. 696–735.

Schegloff, E.A. (2007) *Sequence organization in interaction: a primer in conversation analysis*. Cambridge: Cambridge University Press.

Schegloff, E.A. and Sacks, H. (1973) Opening up closing. *Semiotica* 7: pp. 289–327.

Shulman, L.S. (1987) Knowledge and teaching: foundations of the new reform. *Harvard Educational Review* 57(1): pp. 1–22.

Sinclair, J.M. and Coulthard, M. (1975) *Towards an analysis of discourse: the English used by teachers and pupils*. London: Oxford University Press.

Sukrutrit, P. (2010) *A study of three phases of interaction in synchronous voice-based chatrooms*. PhD Thesis. Newcastle upon Tyne: Newcastle University.

Svennevig, J. (1999) *Getting acquainted in conversation: a study of initial interactions*. Amsterdam: John Benjamins.

Walsh, S. (2006) Talking the talk of the TESOL classroom. *ELT Journal* [online] 60(2): pp. 133–141. Available at: https://academic.oup.com/eltj/article-abstract/60/ 2/133/400304?redirectedFrom=fulltext [Accessed 13 March 2018].

West, C. and Garcia, A. (1988) Conversational shift work: a study of topical transitions between women and men. *Social Problems* [online] 35(5): pp. 551–575. Available at: http://dx.doi.org/10.2307/800615 [Accessed 10 May 2013].

4   Changing a topic

Sample analysis of changing a topic

Maynard (1980), Gardner (1987), Bublitz (1988) and Okamoto and Smith-Lovin (2001) hold a similar notion of topic change – it occurs when a speaker closes an existing topic and replaces it with a completely new topic that has no content connection with the previous topic. Bublitz further adds that when a speaker offers to change a topic and the hearers reject the offer, the speaker is left with only three options: (1) initiating the topic change himself or herself and introducing a new topic, (2) not introducing a new topic but continuing to contribute to the old topic, or (3) neither introducing a new topic nor contributing to the old topic but appealing explicitly or tacitly to the hearer to still hold the speaker role.

Topic change can occur consciously or subconsciously and without the participants being aware of it (Bublitz, 1988). Subconscious topic change is associated with the concept of 'stepwise' topical movement (Sacks, 1992a, p. 561), whereas conscious topic change is associated with 'marked transition' (Sacks, 1992b, p. 352) or what is also known as 'disjunctive topic change' (Holt and Drew, 2005, p. 59). Stepwise movement and marked transition are two processes for closing an old topic, the prerequisite for topic change to occur. Stepwise movement refers to the means by which a topic-in-progress flows naturally into a new, unrelated topic. It does not create a noticeable topic boundary, as the speaker closes the topic implicitly before introducing new topic. This is done by 'connecting' the prior talk to the current talk, even 'though they are different' (Sacks, 1992b, p. 566). Sacks associates the stepwise movement with the quality of a topic:

> In a way, the measure of a good topic is a topic that not so much gets talked of at length, but that provides for transitions to other topics without specific markings that a new topic is going to be done. The richness of a topic is, then, not to be characterized by the fact that there are lots to say about it, but that there are lots of ways to move from it unnoticeably. Whereas a lousy one is one that, the end of it having come, we

know we're at the end of it, and if we're going to go anywhere else we've got to start up again.

(p. 352)

Marked transition, by contrast, refers to the process of introducing a new topic after an old topic has been collaboratively closed by the participants using noticeable strategies. Hence, the topic boundary is visible and realized by all the participants because the topic is terminated by a topic closing sequence.

Closing a topic-in-progress to introduce a new topic can be done by using several strategies. West and Garcia (1988), for instance, highlight two strategies: making contributions and avoiding contributions. The former includes minimal contributions, such as saying *Okay* and *All right* to signal the topic boundary, and the summary of the topic-in-progress; however, the latter includes a series of silences and delayed acknowledgement tokens (e.g. *Um-hmm, mm*). In addition, the participants may also highlight the moral or lesson that can be learned from the topic-in-progress (Schegloff and Sacks, 1973) or give an explicit cue (Bublitz, 1988), such as *Let's talk about something else.*

There are two main reasons that motivate speakers to engage in the action of changing topic (Svennevig, 1999). Once they have accomplished the purpose of a particular topic, they may decide to close the topic and introduce a new topic. This is explained by Sacks (1992b, p. 11) through the metaphor of telling a story. At the very beginning, the teller starts by saying, *I heard the most wonderful thing yesterday,* and when the hearer has heard what the most wonderful thing is, the storytelling has accomplished its purpose and comes to an end.

The second reason to perform the action of changing topic, highlighted by Svennevig (1999), is in response to encountering unexpected trouble during the conversation. As emphasized by Sacks (1992b, p. 352), it is common to find a conversation 'dragging, uninteresting, embarrassing [and] lousy in varieties of ways', and one way to escape is to introduce a new topic. In addition, Bublitz (1988) highlights two typical motivations for a speaker to close a topic: to avoid talking about taboos or something that can damage his or her own image and to avoid talking about something that could harm one of the interlocutors. Jokes and laughter are often used to close the old topic and consequently allow a topic change to occur (Bublitz, 1988; Holt, 2010). The action of changing a topic is summarized in Figure 4.1.

Sample analysis of changing a topic

The actions of changing topics, digressing from topics and shifting topics, are rarely performed on teachers' Timelines. The conversations tend to be short, involving six to seven turns on average, usually only the

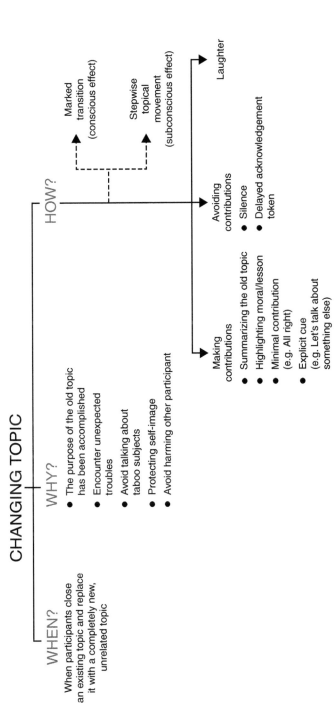

Figure 4.1 Analytical map of topic change

Source: Based on the synthesis of Maynard (1980), Gardner (1987), Bublitz (1988), West and Garcia (1988), Sacks (1992a, 1992b), Svennevig (1999), Okamoto and Smith-Lovin (2001), Holt and Drew (2005), and Holt (2010).

actions of introducing the first topic, continuing the topic and the abrupt closing of the topic. Common ground shared by all the actions of changing topic found is that they are performed towards the end of the conversation, which suggests that teachers do not have enough interest to continue the conversation that deviates from the first topic introduced in the Status update. Hence, it is reasonable to suggest that conversations, albeit informal, are coherent and structured in the sense that the introduction of a new topic often occurs in the Status update rather than in disturbing the flow of the topic-in-progress in the Comment area. The action of changing topic was found in only five out of 178 sets of conversations gathered throughout the entire six-month data collection period. The limited instances of changing the topic on Timelines reflects the high level of support amongst Friends in giving relevant responses to the topic introducers.

The topic change presented in Extract 4.1 is found on Linda's Timeline. She introduces the topic by recounting her experience of being visited by a group of ex-students and expresses her feelings of being touched by the visit. Following the topic introduction, several Comments are left on the Timeline that contribute to the topic continuation before a topic change occurs. The topic is changed by Lily, who introduces a new topic by highlighting that Linda is loved by all her friends (line 4).

Extract 4.1

[Omitted: Three comments that contribute to the continuation of topic]

4   Lily: *Linda* . . . not only students love you . . . friends also love you forever . . .

5   Linda: *Lily* I love u too! Almost 13 years since we last met, right . . . When can we see each other . . . muah to all the way from jb . . .

6   Ija: I also love *Linda!* A very good friend, always helping me who is blurrr . . .

7   Linda: *Ija* it seems to be the other way round now . . . it's u who always help me nowadays! Muah muah. Love u too!

[End of the conversation]

(Linda/SU5/C4–8, translation by the author)

The topic change is initiated by one of the recipients (Lily, line 4) and supported by the first topic introducer (Linda, line 5) who takes up the topic. The new topic is then developed by Ija (line 7). Linda's action of taking up the topic introduced by Lily contributes to the closing of the first topic. If Linda had rejected the newly introduced topic and still talked about the visit by her ex-students and her feeling of being touched, Lily's attempt to introduce a new topic would not have been successful and would have remained a 'speech subject' (Bublitz, 1988, p. 47) or 'side sequence' (Jefferson, 1972, p. 302).

Linda, who introduces the first topic, does not attempt to continue promoting the first topic but allows the topic change to occur. This is perhaps because Lily has initiated the topic change by creating a link between the previous topic and the new topic through the use of the phrase *not only students love you* (line 4). It is only after using this phrase that she introduces the new topic subject *friends also love you forever* (line 4). By doing this, it seems that the new topic has some connection with the previous topic, even though it is no longer about the 'ex-students' visit plus the feeling of being touched by their visit'. In this case, Lily can be said to engage in 'stepwise' topical movement (Sacks, 1992a, p. 561), which enables the topic change to occur subconsciously. Because Linda contributes to the development of the new topic (lines 5 and 8) instead of continuing the first topic that she introduced earlier, it is reasonable to suggest that Linda is unconscious of Lily's attempt to change the topic and therefore does not see any need to appeal for the continuation of the first topic, thus allowing the topic change to occur.

Another possible reason for the topic change succeeding relates to the content of the newly introduced topic in that it concerns the positive qualities of the first topic introducer (Linda), such as being loveable (line 4) and helpful (line 7). It is common in Malay culture that when someone is praised by somebody, they will praise them back, albeit indirectly. For instance, Linda indirectly praises Ija as a helpful friend when she says that Ija always help her nowadays (line 9). Giving praise after being praised leads to the adjacency pair of praising-praising and contributes to the continuation of the newly introduced topic. The continuation of the topic suggests that the teachers are supportive and work collaboratively to construct a good image of one another. Lily and Linda construct each other as loveable individuals (lines 4–6), whilst Linda and Ija work together to construct the identity of a helpful friend (lines 7–9).

Besides employing stepwise topical movement to subconsciously change a particular topic, teachers also change topics in a more explicit way by engaging in a 'marked transition' (Sacks, 1992b, p. 352). The Comments presented in Extract 4.2 are found on Sufi's Timeline. She introduces the topic by expressing her dissatisfaction with the school clerk for making deductions from her salary without informing her first. Sacks points out that participants tend to introduce a new topic when they find the conversation to be 'dragging' and 'uninteresting' (p. 352). It is reasonable to suggest that Lyn introduces the new topic because she finds the conversation to be dragging, as all the 12 prior Comments are written with the same purpose: to calm Sufi down. Thus, Lyn can be said to be attempting to stop the conversation dragging on by introducing a new topic.

Extract 4.2

[Omitted: Four Comments that contribute to the continuation of the first topic]

5	Lyn:	Owh . . . no wonder . . . hehe, fie, have you received the pension scheme letter?
6	Sufi:	not yet . . . coz I just moved that day, process became slow as my personal File reached the new school late . . .
7		n the clerk of this new school did not process the form . . .
8		After a week I completed the form, only then she submitted and even that's because I asked her . . . so not sure when will I get it . . .
9		but Zam already got it
10	Lyn:	I haven't got it too . . . Lan got it . . . huhu
11	Kam:	me too . . . haven't got it

[Omitted: Three Comments that contribute to the continuation of the new topic]

(Sufi/SU11/C5–8, translation by the author)

Lyn introduces the new topic by asking whether Sufi has received the pension scheme letter. She uses the 'minimal contribution strategy', which is the first strategy for closing the topic-in-progress put forth by West and Garcia (1988, p. 556). The minimal contribution here is *Owh . . no wonder* followed by laughter *hehe* (line 5), which is a typical strategy for closing a topic found by many researchers, such as Bublitz (1988) and Holt (2010). Following the topic closure, Lyn introduces the new topic using the 'itemized news inquiry' strategy (Button and Casey, 1985, p. 4), where she asked Sufi about the pension scheme letter.

The marked transition occurs as Lyn makes no attempt to relate the pension scheme letter to the 'deduction of salary by a problematic clerk' highlighted by Sufi in the Status update. Nonetheless, continuing the newly introduced topic, Sufi attempts to redirect the conversation to the first topic in lines 7 and 8, where she points out the inefficiency of the clerk in that the clerk did not process the form (line 7) and submitted the form only after her query (line 8), before she returns to the new topic in line 9. We refer to the strategy of redirecting attention to the first topic whilst at the same time contributing to the continuation of the new topic as a *sandwich* strategy. Using a sandwich strategy to get back to the first topic is not effective, as Lyn and Kam keep talking about the new topic subject, the pension scheme letter. This is perhaps because redirection to the first topic is done implicitly; hence, the participants are perhaps not aware of the attempt.

Analysis of the conversations that go through the actions of introducing, continuing and changing topic leads to the emergence of a more complex conversational pattern than the two patterns identified earlier (see Figure 3.2 in Chapter 3). For instance, prior to the exchange that contributes to the continuation of the new topic between Lyn and Kam, both have had a dyadic conversation with Sufi, who is the first topic introducer. This phenomenon shows that in a long conversation, interactions go further than just being multiple-dyadic conversations between the topic introducer and a recipient but also that they can be dyadic conversations between a recipient and another recipient. This highlights the potential of Facebook Timeline interactions to allow group discussions involving more than two participants, as Friends do interact with one another on Timelines as well as with the Profile owner. The conversational pattern that emerges from the analysis of the topic change in a long conversation is illustrated in Figure 4.2.

Characteristic features of changing a topic on Timelines have emerged from this analysis:

1   The new topic that replaces the first topic introduced in the Status update is rarely developed by the participants, which suggests that the teachers prefer to give Comments that are coherent with the first topic introduced in the Status update rather than talking about something new and unrelated.
2   Both 'stepwise' topical movement (Sacks, 1992a, p. 561) and 'marked transitions' (Sacks, 1992b, p. 352) are employed in the topical action of changing a topic on teachers' Timelines.
3   When engaging in stepwise topical movement, teachers attempt to reduce the level of abruptness of the topic transition by trying to link the old topic with the new topic through the mode of comparison.
4   Similar to topic change in an offline setting, topic changes on teachers' Timelines are initiated either by the first topic introducer or by other

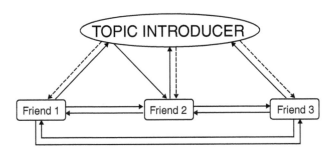

Figure 4.2 A complex conversational pattern observed in long Timeline conversations

recipients. When the change is initiated by the topic introducer, it might mean that he or she has accomplished the intended purpose of introducing the first topic and thus wants to move away from it. When the change is initiated by Friends, it might indicate that they are no longer interested in talking about the first topic.

5   Laughter (e.g. *hehe*) and the avoidance of making contributions are amongst the strategies employed by teachers to close the old topic so that a new topic can be introduced.

6   The first topic introducer may use a *sandwich* strategy to redirect the attention back to the first topic rather than to explicitly reject the recipients' attempts to change the topic.

7   A complex conversational pattern takes place in a long conversation that goes through the three phases of introducing, continuing and changing the topic (see Figure 4.2).

References

Bublitz, W. (1988) *Supportive fellow-speakers and cooperative conversations*. Amsterdam: John Benjamins.

Button, G. and Casey, N. (1985) Topic nomination and topic pursuit. *Human Studies* [online] 8(3): pp. 3–55. Available at: http://dx.doi.org/10.1007%2fBF00143022 [Accessed 6 May 2016].

Gardner, R. (1987) The identification and role of topic in spoken interaction. *Semiotica* 65(1/2): pp. 129–141.

Holt, E. (2010) The last laugh: shared laughter and topic termination. *Journal of Pragmatics* [online] 42(6): pp. 1513–1525. Available at: http://dx.doi.org/10.1016/j.pragma.2010.01.011 [Accessed 12 March 2013].

Holt, E. and Drew, P. (2005) Figurative pivots: the use of figurative expressions in pivotal topic transitions. *Research on Language & Social Interaction* [online] 38(1): pp. 35–61. Available at: http://dx.doi.org/10.1207/s15327973rlsi3801_2 [Accessed 20 March 2013].

Jefferson, G. (1972) Side sequences. In: Sudnow, D.N. (Ed.) *Studies in social interaction*, pp. 294–333. New York: Free Press.

Maynard, D.W. (1980) Placement of topic changes in conversation. *Semiotica* 30: pp. 263–290.

Okamoto, D.G. and Smith-Lovin, L. (2001) Changing the subject: gender, status and the dynamics of topic change. *American Sociological Review* 66(6): pp. 852–873.

Sacks, H. (1992a) *Lectures on conversation volume I*. Oxford: Basil Blackwell.

Sacks, H. (1992b) *Lectures on conversation volume II*. Oxford: Basil Blackwell.

Schegloff, E.A. and Sacks, H. (1973) Opening up closing. *Semiotica* 7: pp. 289–327.

Svennevig, J. (1999) *Getting acquainted in conversation: a study of initial interactions*. Amsterdam: John Benjamins.

West, C. and Garcia, A. (1988) Conversational shift work: a study of topical transitions between women and men. *Social Problems* [online] 35(5): pp. 551–575. Available at: http://dx.doi.org/10.2307/800615 [Accessed 10 May 2013].

5 Digressing from a topic

Sample analysis of digressing from a topic

Topic digression is closely related to topic change. It occurs when 'the speaker's interest in the new topic is at present greater than in the old topic' (Bublitz, 1988, p. 94). Nonetheless, unlike topic change, which occurs after the old topic has been closed by the mutual consent of the interlocutors, topic digression occurs when the current topic has been suspended to allow a new topic to be introduced. After a while, the new topic will be closed, and the suspended old topic will be readopted by the interlocutors. Digressing from a topic can be associated with the concept of 'reinitiating a topic' (Korolija and Linell, 1996, p. 800), topical-level 'back-linking' (Schegloff, 1996, p. 69) and topical-level 'back-connecting' (Local, 2004, p. 377) in the sense that the participants return to the old topic at some point in the conversation. Digressing from a topic is summarized by Bublitz (1988) as follows:

> [T]he speaker SUSPENDS THE current TOPIC, INTRODUCES A new TOPIC (which, at the moment, is of greater interest to him), in due course CLOSES this new TOPIC and READOPTS THE previous, original TOPIC (not yet closed and still holding the interest of the interlocutors).
>
> (p. 95 – original emphasis)

There are several types of digression. The first is what Bublitz (1988, p. 106) terms 'comprehension-securing digression', where interlocutors suspend the current topic to introduce a new topic, which helps the understanding of the previous topic. For instance, when discussing a particular character in a novel, the interlocutors introduce a new topic discussing the conflicts faced by the character and how his handling of the conflicts helps to provide insights into his character. The second is the 'spontaneous digression'. In contrast to the comprehension-securing digression, there is a 'complete lack of any apparent connection' between the topic of the spontaneous digression and the previous topic (Bublitz, 1988, p. 106). This can be taken to imply that spontaneously digressing from a topic shows the speaker has no intention of providing information to develop any understanding of the previous topic.

Digressing from a topic has similarities with the concept of 'side sequence' introduced by Jefferson (1972, p. 302) because both topic digression and side sequence involve the suspension of the topic-in-progress, and the participants later return to the suspended topic. However, in topic digression, the inserted topic is developed into a topic before it is closed so that the speaker can return to the suspended topic, whereas in the side sequence, the inserted topic has not yet settled down as a topic by the time the participants return to the previous topic. This occurs when the participants do not take up the inserted topic, so it remains as a speech subject instead of as a topic subject. In other words, the side sequence is the result of a failed attempt to insert a topic into a topic-in-progress. The topical action of digressing from a topic is summarized in Figure 5.1.

Sample analysis of digressing from a topic

Digressing from a topic is under-researched compared to other topical actions, such as introducing, continuing, shifting and closing the topic. Previous studies (e.g. Foster, 1986; Mentis, Briggs-Whittaker and Gramigna, 1995; Jeon, 2012) tend to have a broad analytical framework, such as introducing, maintaining or progressing and closing the topic; hence, the action of digressing from a topic is rarely scrutinized in detail.

Digressing from a topic is another topical action rarely performed on Timelines. This is surprising because we hypothesized that this topical action would be common due to the way Facebook presents Comments, with only four Comments shown at a time and earlier Comments hidden. Hence, if users want to comment on an old Status update, we hypothesized that they would respond directly to the first topic introduced in the Status update, thus contributing to the action of digressing from a topic, especially if other Friends have inserted a new topic in the earlier Comments. Nonetheless, analysis of the observation data reveals that this phenomenon rarely occurs.

One possible reason for the scarcity of digression from a topic is the length of the conversations, which is usually short, involving only six to seven Comments, on average. For topic digression to occur, the conversation needs to be long enough to go through three phases of topical action – introduction and continuation of the first topic, suspension of the first topic by the introduction and continuation of a new topic and then return to the first topic. Conversations are often closed after the continuation of the first

DIGRESSING FROM A TOPIC

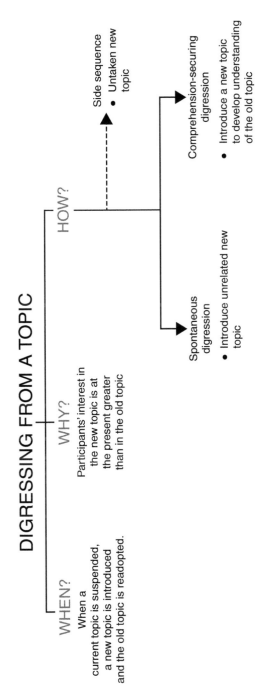

WHEN?

When a current topic is suspended, a new topic is introduced and the old topic is readopted.

WHY?

Participants' interest in the new topic is at the present greater than in the old topic

HOW?

Side sequence
- Untaken new topic

Spontaneous digression
- Introduce unrelated new topic

Comprehension-securing digression
- Introduce a new topic to develop understanding of the old topic

Figure 5.1 Analytical map of topic digression

Source: Based on the synthesis of Bublitz (1988) and Jefferson (1972).

topic, and digression does not occur. Nonetheless, we found two occur-rences of topic digression throughout the six-month observation period, and we analyze the two examples here. We also analyze an example of side sequence in our attempt to show how the side sequence differs from topic digression. We argue that the action of digressing from the first topic reflects teachers' awareness that they need to focus on the first topic intro-duced so that they can signal the presence of structural support to the topic introducer by giving relevant responses. This is because they return to the first topic introduced to make it the focus of the conversation after talking about something else in between.

The first example of topic digression in Extract 5.1 is on Syiba's Time-line. She introduces the first topic by asking for her Friends' opinions of the generalization that all English language teachers have a *wacky* mind and by asking her Friends to confirm that she is an exception. Prior to these Comments are 19 Comments contributing to the development of the first topic.

Extract 5.1

[Omitted: 19 Comments that contribute to the development of the first topic]

20	Nelly:	agree . . . there is one English language teacher at my school, pretty . . .
21		still polite even though she's already a mom to three
22	Syiba:	kah kah kah . . . is she wacky?
23	Nelly:	she is a mom Ariba of course she is no longer wacky . . .
24		it's ok if you want to be wacky now coz you're not yet married . . . hahah . . . i like be your true self . . . wah2
25	Syiba:	eh? Once we become a mom, can no longer be wacky ek? x fun la . . .

[Omitted: Three Comments that contribute to the development of the new topic]

29 Mas: elaborate please what do you mean by wacky

[Omitted: Two Comments that contribute to the continuation of the topic]

(Syiba/SU14/C20–23/C27, translation by the author)

The topic digression shown in Extract 5.1 can be associated with 'comprehension-securing digression' (Bublitz, 1988, p. 106), as there is a high level of connection between the inserted topic and the first topic. Nelly introduces the new topic after she gives a minimal contribution to the first topic by saying *agree* (line 20) to confirm that Syiba is an exception, hence rejecting the generalization that all English language teachers are *wacky*. To make sure her point is understood, she introduces the new topic by highlighting a particular teacher at her school who is *still polite* (line 21), even though she already has three children. Syiba takes up this new topic by showing her interest in knowing more about the particular teacher when she asks whether the teacher is *wacky* (line 22). This question leads to an adjacency pair of question-answer in which Nelly responds by elaborating instead of giving a yes-or-no answer, which contributes to the continuation of the inserted topic (lines 23–24). The return to the first topic, which completes the requirement for topic digression to occur, is discernible when Mas asks Syiba to further clarify the first topic introduced by asking Syiba to elaborate on what she means by *wacky* (line 29).

Based on the analysis of Extract 5.1, a comprehension-securing digression may take the form of an example to help clarify a stance. It becomes a topic because other participants (e.g. Syiba) respond to this specific example, hence leading to exchanges that relate to the subject of the new topic. The new topic is closed when other participants (e.g. Mas) leave Comments that redirect the conversation back to the first topic.

Another interesting point about the topic digression in Extract 5.1 is that it seems to be carried out in a humorous and playful mood. This can be seen from the representation of laughter *kah kah kah* (line 22) instead of the common spelling *hehehe*, which indicates that the level of humour in this segment of conversation is high. The humour is also reflected through Nelly's response *haha, I like* and *wah* (line 24). Nonetheless, Mas, who initiates the return to the first topic, seems to put a halt to this humour by showing a more serious attitude through her question in line 29. Following Mas' question, there are a few Comments (not shown in the extract) that refer to the first topic, which shows that Mas has successfully performed topical-level 'back-linking' (Schegloff, 1996, p. 69). Here a successful return to the old topic in the topical action of digressing from a topic might be determined by the level of seriousness reflected in the Comments that attempt to redirect the focus of the conversation to the original topic.

Extract 5.2 is an example of 'spontaneous digression' (Bublitz, 1988, p. 106), as found on Sufi's Timeline. Sufi introduces the first topic by grumbling about the difficulty in rubbing writing off the old whiteboard used in her classroom.

Extract 5.2

1	Sufi:	I face the same problem!	**Continuing first topic**
2	Fazry:	Do you feel like coming back to the old school? I do.	**Introducing new topic** (The start of the spontaneous digression)
3	Nurul:	I feel like transferring too . . . feel so down . . . demotivated to teach . . .	**Continuing new topic**
4	Sufi:	Fazry, every single day I feel like coming back to jb . . . I thought the old school is too bad already . . . actually here is hell . . .	**Continuing new topic**
		[Omitted: Four Comments that contribute to the continuation of the new topic]	**Continuing new topic**
10	Yana:	need to bring thinner everywhere	**The return to the first topic** (The completion of the spontaneous digression)

[End of the conversation]

(Sufi/SU22/C1–4/C9, translation by the author)

Fazry suspends the old topic using the 'avoiding contribution' strategy and introduces the new topic by inquiring whether Sufi feels like transferring to the old school (line 2). This new topic is first taken up by another Friend (Nurul) in lines 3 and 4 before Sufi further expands the topic in line 5. The return to the first topic is initiated by another Friend (Yana), who suggests one possible solution for Sufi's problem with rubbing the writing off the whiteboard is *to bring thinner* (line 10) with her. A thinner is a solvent used to remove marker pen.

After Yana initiates the return to the first topic, nobody else leaves Comments, not even Sufi, who introduced the first topic. Consequently, the conversation is ended. One explanation for this phenomenon is that the participants' interest is no longer in the first topic. As shown in the extract, the conversation about the new topic is quite lengthy, which suggests that the participants have a high level of interest in talking about the subject of the new topic, which enables them to vent their negative feelings (e.g. lines 3–5). This suggests that venting feelings may attract teachers' attention more than the technical aspects of solving a problem, thus explaining why postings seeking emotional support are found to outnumber other types of postings.

Extract 5.3 is an example of side sequence to show how it differs from topic digression. A side sequence is a failed attempt to introduce a topic where the subject mentioned is not taken up by any other participants. The Comments presented in Extract 5.3 are found on Eisya's Timeline after she introduces the first topic by expressing her shock regarding the policy to make a pass in English compulsory in Sijil Pelajaran Malaysia (Malay for Malaysian Certificate of Education).

Extract 5.3

1	Jaya:	The question is . . . are we ready?	**Continuing topic**
2	Fazry:	I don't think so. Many will fail	**Continuing topic**
3	Jaya:	Definitely! We have many workloads already, no time for extra class!!	**Continuing topic**
4	Eisya:	Agree!	**Continuing topic**
5	Amin:	Sya also remembers you when she listens to this news . . . teacher Eisya	**Continuing topic**
6	Jaid:	timetable is already full with English	**Continuing topic**
7	Eisya:	Bro Amin say Hi to Sis Sya . . . i'm in home sweet home in Bt Pht . . .	**Side sequence**
8	Sue:	end of last year we got survey questions whether should/shouldn't eng be a compulsory subject 2 pass . . . we chose to disagree!!	**Continuing topic**

[Omitted: Four Comments that contribute to the continuation of the first topic]

(Eisya/SU6/C1–8, translation by the author)

The side sequence takes place when Eisya asks Amin to *say Hi to Sis Sya* (line 7). None of the following Comments take up this line. Sue, for instance, who leaves a Comment after Eisya (line 8), links her Comment to the first topic and does not refer to anything in Eisya's Comment in line 7, thus making Eisya's Comment a side sequence.

This chapter has analyzed the actions of digressing from a topic and an example of side sequence:

1 The action of digressing from a topic is a rare phenomenon on teachers' Timelines due to the short length of the conversations. When it occurs, we argue that it reflects the teachers' awareness that they have to redirect the focus of the conversation to the first topic.

2 Even though topic digression rarely takes place, teachers do engage in two types of digression: comprehension-securing digression and spontaneous digression.

3   A comprehension-securing digression may take the form of an example to help clarify a stance.

4   Insertion and the continuation of the new topic may be carried out in a humorous and playful way. When the continuation of the new topic is done in a humorous way, a successful return to the old topic might be determined by the level of seriousness reflected in the Comments that attempt to redirect the focus of the conversation to the previous topic.

5   Greater interest in the new topic might end the old topic, even though an initiation to return to the old topic has been made.

References

Bublitz, W. (1988) *Supportive fellow-speakers and cooperative conversations.* Amsterdam: John Benjamins.

Foster, S.H. (1986) Learning discourse topic management in the preschool years. *Journal of Child Language* [online] 13(2): pp. 231–250. Available at: http://dx.doi.org/10.1017/S0305000900008035 [Accessed 16 June 2013].

Jefferson, G. (1972) Side sequences. In: Sudnow, D.N. (Ed.) *Studies in social interaction*, pp. 294–333. New York: Free Press.

Jeon, S. (2012) *Management of topics in online one-to-one English conversation instruction: a micro-analytic investigation of computer-mediated communication.* PhD Thesis. Newcastle upon Tyne: Newcastle University.

Korolija, N. and Linell, P. (1996) Episodes: coding and analyzing coherence in multiparty conversation. *Linguistics* [online] 34(4): pp. 799–831. Available at: http://dx.doi.org/10.1515/ling.1996.34.4.799 [Accessed 10 June 2013].

Local, J. (2004) Getting back to prior talk and-uh(m) as a back-connecting device in British and American English. In: Couper-Kuhlen, E. and Ford, C.E. (Eds.) *Sound patterns in interaction: cross-linguistic studies from conversation*, pp. 377–401. Amsterdam: John Benjamins.

Mentis, M., Briggs-Whittaker, J. and Gramigna, G.D. (1995) Discourse topic management in senile dementia of the Alzheimer's type. *Journal of Speech and Hearing Research* [online] 38: pp. 1054–1066. Available at: http://dx.doi.org/10.1044/jshr.3805.1054 [Accessed 18 June 2013].

Schegloff, E.A. (1996) Turn organization: one intersection of grammar and interaction. In: Ochs, E., Schegloff, E.A. and Thompson, S.A. (Eds.) *Interaction and grammar*, pp. 53–133. Cambridge: Cambridge University Press.

6   Shifting a topic

Sample analysis of shifting a topic

There are four fundamental features of topic shift as listed by Bublitz (1988, p. 126):

1   the previous topic has not been closed by mutual consent;
2   there is a high connection between the new topic and the previous topic, as a minor speech subject becomes the central topic subject of the new topic;
3   the new topic is at the same hierarchical level as the previous topic in the topic structure of the whole conversation and is therefore taken into account when paraphrasing the conversation to form a discourse topic; and
4   talk about the previous topic is not temporarily suspended and readopted after the talk about the new topic, but the talk about the previous topic is 'de facto' closed by shifting to the new topic.

In addition, Gardner (1987) suggests that topic shift occurs when 'the primary presupposition entailed in the utterances of an exchange cannot be linked to the previous exchange, but can be linked to an earlier exchange which is linked to that previous exchange by topic continuation' (p. 138). In other words, topic shift occurs when the 'speech subject' (marginal and minor subject of the conversation that has not been developed into the topic subject by the interlocutors – see Bublitz, 1988, p. 126) of the earlier utterances becomes the topic subject. What Gardner proposes here is closely related to the second and fourth features of the topic shift highlighted by Bublitz as mentioned in the previous list.

Gardner's (1987) three subtypes of topic shift are also closely related to the fundamental features of shifting a topic proposed by Bublitz (1988). According to Gardner, the first type of topic shift occurs when the speaker 'pick[s] up the thread from an earlier exchange within the current sequence' after a 'topic has come to a dead end' (p. 139). This is related to Bublitz's fourth fundamental feature; the previous topic is 'de facto' closed by the shift to the new topic (p. 126). Gardner's second type of topic shift is 'topic shading', when the domain of the topic is expanded, such as from talking about the 'date of a forthcoming exam' to talking about the 'forthcoming exam' (p. 139). This type of topic shift is related to Bublitz's second fundamental feature, as there is a high degree of connectedness between the previous and the new topic; one aspect of the topic subject is expanded to form another topic subject.

Gardner's (1987) third type of topic shift is called 'topic fading', when 'there is avoidance of one aspect of the topic' (pp. 136–137), such as from talking about 'students plus extra classes' to 'teachers plus extra classes'. This third type of topic shift cannot be associated with any of Bublitz's (1988) fundamental features of topic shift except that both the previous and the new topics need to be taken into account when reporting the discourse topic; hence, Gardner's notion of 'avoiding one aspect of the topic' is added to the list of fundamental features of topic shift for a comprehensive analytical framework for examining the data in this study.

Besides Gardner (1987) and Bublitz (1988), Linell and Korolija (1997) also contributed to the literature on topic shift in face-to-face conversations. Linell and Korolija propose topical episode analysis (TEA) as a coding system for analyzing topic shift and suggest eight strategies for initiating the topic shift. To achieve a more comprehensive framework, we combined TEA with Bublitz's fundamental features of topic shift and Gardner's types of topic shift. An episode, according to Linell and Korolija, consists of a minimum of three turns, and two of the three need to be uttered by different speakers. Based on this perspective, analyzing the Timeline interaction using the four-sequence exchange, as explained in Chapter 1, seems to be appropriate as it covers a single episode of the conversations.

The eight strategies for initiating topic shift as noted by Linell and Korolija (1997) are summarized next:

1   Recontextualizing an element from the prior episode, where a particular aspect or element – typically mentioned towards the end of the prior episode – is taken as a starting point for the new episode and consequently put into a new context. We refer to this strategy as *topic recontextualizing*. According to Linell and Korolija, recontextualization can be either (1) recontextualization via an association to 'a fact, a concept, or a referent' peripherally mentioned in the prior episode, or (2) recontextualization via metalinguistic comments in 'the form or meaning of some expressions' mentioned in the prior episode (p. 176).

2   Providing an analogous episode to a prior episode in which the participants might initiate a story, recount an experience or an argument with

the same point as the one in the prior episode. We refer to this strategy as *topic analogizing*.

3 Returning to a prior, non-adjacent topic in the same discourse. This strategy is excluded in the analytical framework of topic shift because it is synonymous with digressing from a topic, as discussed in Chapter 5.

4 Referring to an event taking place in the situation, when the participants are attracted to something that is happening in the immediate environment and start talking about it. We argue this strategy is most likely to be employed by participants in face-to-face conversation when they suddenly notice something, such as students fighting or students involved in an accident, and therefore is not applicable to Timeline conversation because the participants are not in the same location during the course of the conversation.

5 When the participants start to talk about the person or an object present in the situation. Linell and Korolija associate this strategy with 'sensitivity of the object', such as when participants notice something wrong with the physical aspect of another participant (p. 185). Because this study involves online conversation where the participants do not physically see one another, we excluded this strategy from the analytical framework of topic shift in Timeline conversations.

6 Taking up a predefined, agenda-bound topic or subactivity in which the participants take up a point for discussion from an agenda that is previously known to the participants in the conversation. This strategy is more likely to be employed in formal conversations – for example, with agendas – that is, 'all the cases in institutional, task-oriented discourse', where participants know beforehand what can or will be brought up and when to nominate a particular topic (Linell and Korolija, 1997, p. 188). Because Timeline conversations do not have a predefined agenda known to all the Friends who might join in the conversation, we excluded this strategy from the analytical framework of topic shift adopted in this study. Even if the Timeline conversations have a predefined agenda, and the participants return to this agenda during the conversation, they are engaging in digressing from a topic rather than shifting a topic.

7 Invoking other topics that are situationally near at hand (belonging to situationally activated background assumptions), whereby the participants engage in four activities: (1) commenting on the social situation in general, (2) exploring one another's relevant biographies, (3) invoking items from a common biography, and (4) invoking topics about absent members' activities. We argue that this strategy is not exclusive to the initiation of topic shift because for a topic shift to occur, Bublitz (1988) emphasizes that there should be a significant connection between the

new and the previous topic. Unless the previous topic relates to any of the four main activities highlighted, we argue that this strategy cannot be seen as an attempt to initiate topic shift.

8   Contextually unanchored episodes in which the participants introduce a new topic that has no connection to the topics of prior episodes and is not anchored in the situation or based on common knowledge. This strategy is excluded in the analytical framework of topic shift because it is a characteristic of changing a topic.

Two out of the eight strategies for initiating topic shift proposed by Linell and Korolija (1997) are relevant to the concept of topic shift adopted in this book. The two strategies are what we refer to as *topic recontextualizing* and *topic analogizing*, and these strategies are combined with Bublitz's (1988) and Gardner's (1987) notions of topic shift. The synthesized analytical mapping to examine topic shift on Timelines is summarized in Figure 6.1.

Sample analysis of shifting a topic

Comparatively speaking, the action of shifting topic is more common on teachers' Timelines than changing and digressing from a topic. One possible reason is that unlike topic digression, topic shifts can take place in a short conversation. For instance, after the second or third Comments that continue the first topic, the participants might engage either consciously or unconsciously in the action of shifting topic. Topic shift might occur unconsciously due to the subtle difference between the new topic and the old topic, and consequently the participant who initiates the topic shift might not be viewed by other participants as deviating from the first topic in the Status update because there is a high level of connectivity between the two topics.

The majority of the topic shifts on teachers' Timelines take the form of topic analogizing and, to a lesser extent, topic recontextualizing. Gardner's (1987) 'topic fading' and 'topic shading' (p. 139) are very rare in that only one occurrence of each type was found. When engaging in topic analogizing, teachers recount their own experiences, which has the same point as in the previous exchange and reflects teachers' high level of interest in sharing experiences with one another on Timelines. More interestingly, the experiences recounted often have different contexts because the teachers are geographically distributed. Extract 6.1 is used to closely examine an example of topic analogizing found on teachers' Timelines. It is taken from Sufi's Timeline, and the Comments are the responses to her Status update when she introduces the first topic by grumbling about colleagues' attitudes during a school meeting over breakfast at the canteen.

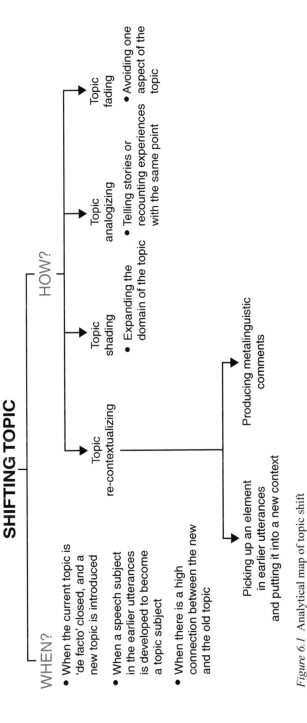

SHIFTING TOPIC

WHEN?

- When the current topic is 'de facto' closed, and a new topic is introduced
- When a speech subject in the earlier utterances is developed to become a topic subject
- When there is a high connection between the new and the old topic

HOW?

Topic re-contextualizing

Producing metalinguistic comments

Picking up an element in earlier utterances and putting it into a new context

Topic shading
- Expanding the domain of the topic

Topic analogizing
- Telling stories or recounting experiences with the same point

Topic fading
- Avoiding one aspect of the topic

Figure 6.1 Analytical map of topic shift

Source: Based on the synthesis of Gardner (1987), Bublitz (1988), and Linell and Korolija (1997).

Extract 6.1

[Omitted: Four Comments that contribute to the continuation of the topic]

5	Fazry:	they have not been eating for weeks! lol	**Continuing topic**
6	Sufi:	as if they are going to die if they skipped the breakfast.	**Continuing topic**
7	Barnett:	the stomach is much more important than the meeting . . . haha	**Shifting topic (Analogizing)**
8		same thing here many do not attend assembly just because they want to eat first	
9	Sue:	my school is the most efficient since the canteen is beside the open hall where the assembly takes place . . .	**Shifting topic (Analogizing)**
10		who dares not to attend the assembly? haha	
11	Linda:	at my school thank god . . . they don't dare to come late to meeting.	**Shifting topic (Analogizing)**
12		The principal is very fierce. He can reprimand teachers just like that	
13	Sufi:	hahah. Deserve them well	

[Omitted: Five Comments that contribute to the continuity of the topic]

(Barnett/SU13/C5–10, translation by the author)

Barnett, Sue and Linda engage in topic analogizing by telling their own 'story' with the same theme as the first topic, which is 'teachers' attitudes plus their empty stomachs'. Here Sufi and other Friends who read this conversation are presented with two different scenarios by the participants. Barnett recounts a similar phenomenon in her school where teachers' tend to compromise their responsibilities in order to eat (lines 7–8), hence suggesting to Sufi that she is not the only one who has experienced the problem. In contrast, Sue and Linda use their stories to highlight a different scenario at school where teachers cannot ignore their responsibilities, even if they want to, due to certain factors (lines 9–12).

The 'second stories' (Sacks, 1992, p. 11) unfolded by Barnett, Sue and Linda have important functions in this conversation. By suggesting to Sufi that she is not the only one who has this experience, Barnett can be seen as trying to send a 'you're not alone' message to Sufi; hence, she should not feel afflicted by the problem. It is reasonable to suggest that the 'connection' that Barnett is trying to establish serves as a form of emotional support to Sufi as well as the symbol of a shared identity between them. This is because Barnett could have responded differently – for instance, by challenging Sufi's observation that the teachers might not attend the school meeting because they are unaware of it and not because they prioritize their empty stomachs. Instead Barnett chooses to tell a story that seems to support Sufi's observation.

On the other hand, Sue and Linda's stories enable Sufi to see the problem from a different perspective. Instead of grumbling about the same problem, Sue and Linda indirectly put forth a more positive view, that it can be controlled if the canteen is beside the open hall (line 9) and the principal is firmer in managing the teachers (line 12). The second stories contributed by Sue and Linda might have a positive influence on Sufi's (as well as other Friends who read this conversation) professional lives because it helps her see the problem from a new perspective. In other words, the Comments from Sue and Linda allow Sufi to engage in reflection. As highlighted by Hargreaves and Fullan (1992), personal stories are a useful resource for teacher professional development in the sense that they help 'teachers articulate their voices as a way of constructing and reconstructing the purposes and priorities in their work, both individually and collectively' (p. 5).

In terms of topic transition, Barnett has been careful in shifting topic so that the transition is very subtle. This is done by producing a short comment, *the stomach is much more important than the meeting* (line 7), which contributes to the continuation of the first topic, followed by laughter *haha* (line 7) to de facto close the first topic, and starts shifting the topic by telling her own story of teachers who do not attend assembly just because they want to eat first (line 8). There are three occurrences of *haha* in this extract, all of which are positioned differently by the participants: in the middle of the Comment (line 7), at the end of the Comment (line 10) and at the beginning of the Comment (line 13). Even though researchers of spoken discourse associate laughter with turn-opening (e.g. Evison, 2013), that laughter on Timelines is used for three different purposes: to link the utterances (line 7), as a turn-closer (line 10) and as a turn-opener (line 13).

Extract 6.2 illustrates another type of topic shift, which is topic recontextualizing. The example is taken from Syiba's Timeline. She introduces the first topic in the Status update by recounting her experience of punishing a student who made fun of her in the classroom.

Extract 6.2

[Omitted: Two Comments that contribute to the continuation of the first topic]

3	Barnett:	should give a more severe punishment.	**Continuing topic**
4	Syiba:	I will, if he doesn't change.	**Continuing topic**
5	Zul:	tell the student 'I scold you in human language you laugh . . . starting from today, I'll call you bitch'. . . it works	**Shifting topic** (The start of topic recontextualization)
6	Shila:	your language is so foul . . . hehehe . . . I once told my form 4 students . . . "you all human or animal? Why so stupid?!". . . can you see the use of the northern dialect there? Hehe	
7		when I am angry I use northern dialect	
8	Zul:	bitch and animal are similar!	(The end of topic recontextualization)
9	Lyn:	that surely works . . .	

[Omitted: Six Comments that contribute to the topic continuity]
(Syiba/SU3/C3–8, translation by the author)

The topic recontextualization is initiated by Shila in line 6, who produces a metalinguistic Comment as a response to Zul's suggestion in line 5. Shila directly tells Zul that his language is *so foul*, suggesting that it is inappropriate to be used in the classroom. The laughter *hehehe* (line 6) that follows the direct comment can be seen as an attempt to tone down her criticism of Zul's advice. Interestingly, Shila then announces that she once called her students *animals*, but she said it in northern dialect. Here it appears that Shila is trying to suggest that calling students *bitch* in English sounds inappropriate, but it is more acceptable if teachers use the word *animal* and say it in a particular dialect so it sounds more like a joke. The negotiation that occurs between Shila and Zul leads to the emergence of metalinguistic Comments and consequently recontextualizes the first topic.

Producing metalinguistic Comments might enable the teachers to engage in informal learning, albeit they are unconscious of the learning process. As seen in Extract 6.2, teachers are negotiating what terms of reference are appropriate and what are not in the classroom. Using appropriate language when talking to students is crucial as they are English language teachers. Hence, it is reasonable to suggest that producing metalinguistic comments by discussing the appropriateness of the language used in school on Timelines may contribute to the development of teachers' professional lives.

Extract 6.3 illustrates another strategy of recontextualizing a topic, which is associating the new topic to a concept or referent mentioned in the previous exchange. The extract is taken from Sufi's Timeline, and the conversation occurs after Sufi introduces the first topic by announcing that her body is still shaking because of her anger towards problematic students.

Extract 6.3

[Omitted: Two Comments that contribute to the topic continuation]

3	Fazry:	. . . a challenging life of a teacher . . . huhu	**Continuing topic**
4	Barnett:	be strong k?	**Continuing topic**
5	Sufi:	emm *Barnett* seems like I can get heart attack if I hv to face d same situation daily . . .	**Shifting topic** (The start of topic recontextualization)
6		its like talking to a mental person . . . the more you scold them, the more they laugh	
7	Barnett:	if they seem to be mental, just ignore . . . the more you entertain them, the more painful you feel . . .	
8	Sufi:	right, entertaining mental students can make us go mental	
9	Jaz:	dangerous oooo. They could do anything to you	(The end of topic recontextualization)

[Omitted: Three Comments that contribute to the continuity of the topic]
(Sufi/SU3/C3–8, translation by the author)

The topic recontextualizing is initiated by Barnett (line 7), who takes up the concept of *mental person* (pejoratively referring to someone who is mentally ill) mentioned by Sufi (line 6). The recontextualization is then developed by Sufi and Jaz, who leave Comments related to *mental person* (lines 8–9). Barnett initiates the topic recontextualization by advising Sufi to ignore the *mental* student, as she believes that it will only make Sufi's life *painful*. Barnett's advice here reflects her concern for Sufi, which we argue should be seen as evidence of a sense of belonging and an attempt to construct emotional support. Even though this is unrequested advice, Sufi seems to accept it with an open heart when she agrees that entertaining *mental* students can make teachers *go mental* (line 8). This finding is interesting as it contradicts the finding found by many researchers that uninvited advice could lead to disputes. For instance, Sillence (2010) reveals that members of online health communities often have to deal with uncongenial advice from other members, and they have to use discursive techniques, such as humour, to avoid disputes. In addition, the advice seekers value the advice given by like-minded members more than that from others. Sillence explores how people manage the process of advice-giving in an online cancer support group, where the members might not be people who the participants know offline. This is in contrast to Facebook, where users are mostly connected with people they have some level of connection to offline.

Extract 6.4 is an example of another form of topic shift, 'topic shading' (Gardner, 1987, p. 139). Topic shading occurs when a topic is expanded, such as from talking about the 'date of the forthcoming exam' to 'the forthcoming exam' more generally. This extract shows how the topic is expanded from talking about the 'students' misbehaviour plus its effects on teachers' professional lives' to 'teachers' professional lives'. It is taken from Zeti's Timeline and is the response to her Status update where she introduces the first topic by grumbling about students, whom she sees as spoilt brats, and expresses her concern that teachers will be blamed if the students do not score high marks in the exam.

Extract 6.4

[Omitted: Three Comments that contribute to the continuation of the first topic]

4	Syiba:	people always blame us for students' misbehaviour	**Continuing topic**
5	Fazry:	and policy makers only want one thing – students pass the exam with flying colours.	**Continuing topic**
6	Azi:	they don't give a damn . . . if the result is bad, teachers who need to attend courses!	**Continuing topic**
7	Linda:	thought attending courses is our responsibility as a teacher? Heee	**Shifting topic** (The start of topic shading)
8	Nur:	agree with *Linda*. Take the courses as an opportunity to gain knowledge, for us to be a better teacher. Chaiyok!	

9	Azi:	we teachers work hard like crazy . . .	(The end of topic shading)

[Omitted: Two Comments that contribute to the continuity of the topic]
(Zeti/SU2/C4–9, translation by the author)

Azi's Comment (line 6) is the last Comment that contributes to the about-ness of the first topic, 'students' misbehaviour plus its effects on teachers' professional lives'. Linda and Nur, who leave Comments after Azi, engage in topic shading by expanding the topic to talk about teachers' professional lives in general. Linda, who initiates the topic shading, challenges Azi's Comment that teachers need to attend courses because students' results are bad (line 6). Linda proposes a different perspective, that attending courses is the teachers' responsibility (line 7), and this is supported by Nur, who encourages Azi to take the courses as an opportunity to gain knowledge (line 8). Interestingly, Azi, who is challenged by Linda and given unre-quested advice by Nur, does not show any sign of anger in her Comment (line 9), which suggests a strong sense of belonging amongst them. Per-haps this is also because Linda has successfully helped Azi to 'repair' her interpretation (Botschner, 2000, p. 10) that attending courses should not be regarded as a burden but as an opportunity to learn.

Extract 6.5 illustrates the last type of topic shift, 'topic fading' (Gard-ner, 1987, p. 139). Topic fading takes place when participants avoid talking about one aspect of the topic, such as talking about 'students plus extra classes' and switching to 'teacher plus extra classes'. The extract is taken from Syiba's Timeline, and it presents the Comments on her Status update where she introduces the first topic by highlighting the unintended con-sequences that might arise when the government allows students to bring mobile phones to school. Topic fading occurs when the teachers shift the focus of their discourse from 'student elopement plus mobile phone-related policy' to 'teachers' stress plus mobile phone-related policy'. Prior to these Comments, the teachers talked about how student elopement problems could become worse if they are allowed to bring mobile phones to school.

Extract 6.5

[Omitted: 18 Comments that contribute to the continuity of the first topic]

19	Zeti:	It will be easier for the students to text their partners and then elope after school	**Continuing topic**
20	Syiba:	. . . and someone up there cannot even foresee this unintended consequence!	**Continuing topic**

21	Sya:	huhuhu many teachers will suffer from high blood pressure soon.	**Shifting topic** (The start of topic fading)
22		stressed of controlling students that bring handphones . . . hazardous	
23	Jebat:	better to take care of goats compared to students, haha . . . teachers don't get angry yea . . .	
24	Syiba:	who knows super-impulse porn photos of teachers might exist soon . . . like celebrities . . . hahaha . . .	
25	Sya:	we young teachers can reprimand students if they are too much into their hp.	
26		Old teachers, will they have the courage to fight with the students?	

[Omitted: Six Comments that contribute to the continuity of the topic]
(Syiba/SU11/C19–24, translation by the author)

The topic fading is initiated by Sya, who gives a minimal response to the previous exchange through her *huhuhu* (line 21) before she starts to shift the talk to focus on how teachers can be affected by the policy that allows students to bring mobile phones to school. She infers that many teachers will suffer from high blood pressure (line 21). Jebat's Comment is rather general; there is not enough information to say whether her Comment is a response to Sya's Comment (lines 21–22) or to the earlier Comments about the student elopement problem. We argue that it is the generality of Jebat's Comment that makes the topic of teachers' stress introduced by Sya seem to be taken up and that encourages Syiba (line 24) and Sya (lines 25–26) to further develop the topic. If Jebat had given a more specific Comment related to the student elopement problem, Sya might not have been successful in initiating topic fading, as Jebat redirects the conversation to focus on the student elopement problem. In that case, Sya's Comment (lines 21–22) is only a side sequence. Even though it is unclear whether Sya, Jebat and Syiba are talking to one another as a group or simply taking part in a dyadic conversation (e.g. Sya-Syiba, Jebat-Syiba), the four Comments seem to be coherent, focusing on the effects of the mobile phone-related policy on teachers' lives, hence contributing to topic fading.

This chapter has shown how the teachers engage in the act of shifting topic:

1   Topic shift occurs more frequently on Timelines than changing and digressing from a topic, most probably because topic shift can take place more easily in short conversations.

2   Similar to face-to-face conversation, teachers engage in stepwise topical movements and marked transitions when shifting topic.

3   Topic analogizing is the main form of topic shift on Timelines, followed by topic recontextualizing. Topic fading and topic shading occur occasionally.

4   Topic analogizing enables teachers to exchange their 'second stories' (Sacks, 1992, p. 11), which we argue is an attempt to co-construct emotional support, besides broadening teachers' perspectives, because the stories have different settings due to the teachers' wide geographical distribution.

5   Topic recontextualizing through the use of metalinguistic Comments enables teachers to negotiate the appropriateness of their language use and contributes to the development of their professional identity.

6   Advice-seeking and advice-giving emerging through the analysis of topic shift reveals that teachers tend to accept unrequested advice rather than to dispute it, which reflects a strong sense of belonging.

7   Vague previous Comments might contribute to topic shift, especially when the participants infer that the Comments are contributing to the new topic rather than to the old topic.

References

Botschner, J. (2000) *Doing not providing: a discourse analytic investigation of social support as a responsive process*. Ontario: University of Guelph Press.

Bublitz, W. (1988) *Supportive fellow-speakers and cooperative conversations*. Amsterdam: John Benjamins.

Evison, J. (2013) Turn openings in academic talk: where goals and roles intersect. *Classroom Discourse* [online] 4(1): pp. 3–26. Available at: http://dx.doi.org/10.1 080/19463014.2013.783499 [Accessed 13 April 2014].

Gardner, R. (1987) The identification and role of topic in spoken interaction. *Semiotica* 65(1/2): pp. 129–141.

Hargreaves, A. and Fullan, M.G. (1992) Introduction. In: Hargreaves, A. and Fullan, M.G. (Eds.) *Understanding teacher development*, pp. 1–19. London: Cassell.

Linell, P. and Korolija, N. (1997) Coherence in multi-party conversation: episodes and contexts in interaction. In: Givon, T. (Ed.) *Conversation: cognitive, communicative and social perspectives*, pp. 167–205. Amsterdam: John Benjamins.

Sacks, H. (1992) *Lectures on conversation volume I*. Oxford: Basil Blackwell.

Sillence, E. (2010) Seeking out very like-minded others: exploring trust and advice issues in an online health support group. *International Journal of Web Based Communities* [online] 6(4): pp. 376–394. Available at: http://dx.doi.org/10.1504/ IJWBC.2010.035840 [Accessed 10 July 2014].

7 Closing a topic

Sample analysis of closing a topic

Bublitz (1988) highlights three typical ways of closing a topic. Firstly, a topic is closed at the end of the conversation, and this is a topical action in its own right. Secondly, a topic is closed as part of the more complex topical action of changing the topic, when the participants 'break off' the topic in 'a very direct and marked way' (p. 133). Bublitz's concept of breaking off a topic is similar to Sacks' (1992) concept of marked transition, which does not occur with the interlocutors' mutual consent, and there is no strong connection between the previous and the new topics in terms of content. Thirdly, a topic may be closed as a 'consequence and by-product' of topic shift and topic digression in which the interlocutors finally 'lose sight' of the previous topic (p. 133). We have reviewed how a topic is closed during a conversation as part of the more complex topical actions of changing a topic (Chapter 4), digressing from a topic (Chapter 5) and shifting from a topic (Chapter 6). Hence, this chapter will focus on topic closure at the end of a conversation.

Closing a topic at the end of a conversation is thoroughly discussed by Schegloff and Sacks (1973) and Placencia (1997) and is characterized as a complex action. Schegloff and Sacks argue that speakers need to 'organize the simultaneous arrival of the conversationalists at a point where one speaker's completion will not occasion another speaker's talk, and that will not be heard as some speaker's silence' (pp. 294–295). This is because if another speaker continues talking after one speaker's completion, or interprets the silence as a strategy to offer the floor to other speakers, the conversation will never come to an end if the machinery for turn-taking does not come to a stop. Therefore, the participants need to signal their desire to bring the conversation to an end (Placencia, 1997) so that others will take the appropriate action to help end the conversation. This contributes to the understanding that conversations are brought to a close through the collaboration of the participants.

Schegloff and Sacks (1973) suggest two types of procedures employed by participants to initiate closure: pre-closure and terminal exchange. Within the category of pre-closing devices, Schegloff and Sacks point out the concept of 'warrants', utterances, such as *okay*, *well* and *so*, produced alone, that are permits for closing (p. 306). The concept of warrants is synonymous with the concept of 'phrases of non-commitment' introduced by Bublitz (1988), such as *that may be*, *I should not wonder* and *that's that* (p. 131). Besides the warrants in the form of minimal utterances, Bublitz expands the scope of warrants to include a summary of what has been said about the topic, a paraphrase of it, the conclusion, the evaluation and the moral stated by the participants. In addition to the concept of warrants, Schegloff and Sacks also suggest the concept of 'announcements' whereby participants clearly state their intentions to terminate the conversation. Within the category of terminal exchange, they highlight how conversations are closed by the production of pairs of utterances, such as *thank you – you're welcome*, and farewell sequences, such as *bye – bye*, which mark the end of a conversation. The action of topic closure is summarized in Figure 7.1.

Sample analysis of closing a topic

This section focuses on topic closure at the end of the conversation because topic closure in the course of a conversation has been discussed as the topical action of changing topic, when the old topic needs to be closed before the introduction of the new topic (Chapter 4). Closing the topic during the conversation on teachers' Timelines is similar to topic closure during face-to-face conversation, whereby teachers engage in stepwise topical movement for a subtle topic transition and boundaried movement for a more marked transition. In terms of the strategies employed to close the topic, teachers use either minimal contribution or avoiding contribution strategies.

Closing the topic at the end of Timeline conversations exhibits distinctive features. It does not share the characteristics of topic closure in dialogic face-to-face or telephone conversations. Schegloff and Sacks' (1973) pre-closing and terminal exchanges are not applied by teachers when closing their Timeline conversations. It is done abruptly by teachers who avoid contributing to the last Comment, even though the Friend who leaves the last Comment requires a response from them. To illustrate this phenomenon, Extract 7.1 presents the last four-sequence exchange in a conversation initiated by Wafi where she introduced the first topic by presenting two identical sentences and asked her Friends which sentence is grammatically correct.

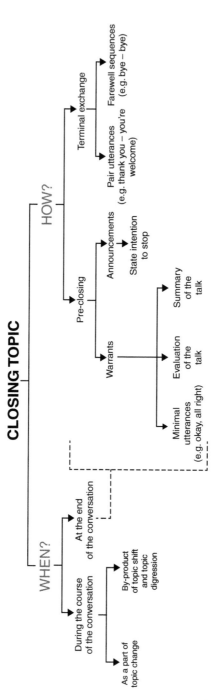

Figure 7.1 Analytical map of topic closure

Source: Based on the synthesis of Schegloff and Sacks (1973), Bublitz (1988), Sacks (1992), and Placencia (1997).

Closing a topic 65

Extract 7.1

[Omitted: 18 Comments that contribute to the continuity of the first topic]

19	Zara:	i'll ask my sifu . . . wait for his answer k.
20	Matt:	hesitant is an adj n hesitate is a verb.i never use 'hesitated' before.
21		as i know, there are only seven verb be . . . am, is, are, was, were, been, and being.
22		for me, both sentences seems wrong . . .
23		so i suggest you change those sentences to "Don't hesitate to see the teacher on duty"
24	Matt:	remember what our lecturers said about teaching grammar . . . "PLAY SAFE"
25	Zara:	the answer from Santa Maria-Shouldn't it be 'don't hesitate to . . .' although A is also correct.
26		Hesitate to do something cannot be used in the passive form as it is intransitive therefore the adjective hesitant must be used instead.
27		Does that sound convincing?

[End of the conversation]

(Wafi/SU2/C19–22)

Both Zara and Matt are interested in continuing the topic introduced by Wafi. Matt, for instance, shows his interest by giving elaborated responses in that he leaves Comments twice (lines 20–24), whereas Zara shows her interest by turning to another expert (Santa Maria) and rejoins the conversation with an elaborated response (lines 25–27). Even after giving an explanation, she asks Wafi whether it sounds *convincing* (line 27). If Wafi responded saying she was not convinced by that explanation, Zara might have come up with another explanation and continued the topic. Hence, in this case, Wafi can be said to employ an avoiding contribution strategy to close the topic at the end of the conversation.

It is interesting to see that Wafi does not comment or give any 'warrants' (Schegloff and Sacks, 1973, p. 306) for her to close the conversation that she initiated. To apply Schegloff and Sacks' procedure, Wafi could have engaged in pre-closing by giving warrants, for instance, *okay* or *thank you*, but she chooses not to do so. Schegloff and Sacks argue that closing the topic at the end of the conversation needs to be done carefully so as not to terminate the relationship between the participants. By not responding to Zara's question and offering no warrant to close the conversation, Wafi cannot be said to have closed the conversation carefully. Nonetheless, it does not terminate their friendship, as Zara and Wafi are later found to still be engaging in the co-construction of support related to different topics (not shown here).

Topic closure at the end of Timeline conversations that occurs without any warrants or terminal exchange might relate to the nature of the conversation, that it is permanently recorded on Timelines, unless the first topic introducer deletes the Status update, which will also delete the entire conversation. Because it will be left available on the Timelines, the conversation might continue again if anyone in the Friends list scrolls down the Timelines and leaves new Comments in future. Therefore, ending the conversation without having a marked closure enables the conversation to be reinitiated when other Friends have something interesting to contribute to the topic. This is not impossible as when a new Comment is made on the old Status updates. It will appear in the users' current News Feeds, hence giving a sense of newness to the old conversation. In this sense, teachers have the opportunity 'to come back' to old conversations with new perspectives and to reshape their understanding of particular issues.

The analysis of topic closure on teachers' Timelines has led to the emergence of the new characteristics of topic closure at the end of conversations:

1   Pre-closure and terminal exchanges are not applied in closing the topic at the end of a Timeline conversation because the closure occurs abruptly.
2   Topic closure can occur through avoiding contribution strategies, whereby teachers simply stop leaving Comments.
3   A topic might be closed by the topic introducer, even though other Friends still show interest in the topic, which reflects the topic introducer's power to control the conversation.
4   Not having a marked closure might enable the conversation to be reinitiated again in future, which provides an opportunity for teachers to discuss an old topic from new perspectives.

References

Bublitz, W. (1988) *Supportive fellow-speakers and cooperative conversations.* Amsterdam: John Benjamins.

Placencia, M.E. (1997) Opening up closings: the Ecuadorian way. *TEXT: An Interdisciplinary Journal for the Study of Discourse* [online] 17(1): pp. 53–81. Available at: http://dx.doi.org/10.1515/text.1.1997.17.1.53 [Accessed 10 May 2013].

Sacks, H. (1992) *Lectures on conversation volume II.* Oxford: Basil Blackwell.

Schegloff, E.A. and Sacks, H. (1973) Opening up closing. *Semiotica* 7: pp. 289–327.

Index

Note: figures are denoted with italicized page numbers.